Get Busy Living

Managing Sexuality Intelligently

by

Steven Ing, M.A., M.F.T.

© ING Intellectual, Inc., 2016

The author gratefully acknowledges Anthony Cotterell's contributions to this manual.

ALL RIGHTS RESERVED UNDER INTERNATIONAL AND PAN-AMERICAN COPYRIGHT CONVENTIONS. PUBLISHED IN THE UNITED STATES OF AMERICA BY GIANT PUBLISHING, TUCSON, ARIZONA.

© 2016 ING INTELLECTUAL, INC.

Cover Design by Nicole Rose Dion

ISBN-10: 1-933975-03-2

ISBN-13: 978-1-933975-03-0

10 9 8 7 6 5 4 3 2 1

FOR MORE INFORMATION, PLEASE VISIT:

WWW.STEVENING.COM

Preface

This manual is designed to help you progress through your program. You will find it helpful if you use it honestly and openly. The handbook will be regularly updated as needed and if you have an idea which will help others, please suggest it. The thoughts and techniques expressed in this handbook come out of years of experience of therapists and clients in the program. We welcome you to become a part of that process of healing in our community.

Throughout the handbook you will find comments or suggestions made by others who have gone before you. The comments come from the minds of those with a lot of experience and an intention to help you. Particularly worthy of thanks is Word Work for editing this manual. Thank you to the men and women in the program who have inspired and tested these thoughts and even made contributions to it (Joby, Leland and Darrel). Your contributions to our community's health and safety are greatly appreciated.

Lastly, we know that family members and loved ones may read this manual out of mere curiosity, personal need or simply out of a great love for you. We welcome such examination and have written some parts of the manual with significant others in mind. These parts of the manual will inform them about your process in treatment and your progress over time. We hope their understanding of your work will help you in your progress toward success. Feel free to makes notes in your manual.

> *"Every man is my superior in some way, but there is also some way in which I am superior to each individual I meet. When I am able to recognize, accept and honor that superiority in others— not in some general way, but individually, then I am on the path to being a whole person."*
>
> L. L.

Your notes here:

Table of Contents

Preface i
Table of Contents ii
Introduction to Your Program 1
Program Orientation 3
Our Commitments to You 4
For Family and Loved Ones 5
Overview of Treatment Goals 7
How to Ruin Your Treatment 10

Part I—The Need to Change

Chapter 1 . . . Changing My Thoughts 13
    Step 1—The Need for Sexual Information 14
    Step 2—The Need for Clear Thinking 17
    Step 3—The Need to Embrace My Failure 20

Chapter 2 . . . Changing My Heart 23
    Step 4—The Need to Disclose 24
    Step 5—The Need for a New Heart 27
    Step 6—The Need for Integrity 30
    Step 7—The Need for Compassion 33

Chapter 3 . . . Changing My Ways 36
    Step 8—The Need for Friendship 38
    Step 9—The Need to Make Things Right 42
    Step 10—The Need to Understand the Past 46
    Step 11—The Need for Success 50
    Step 12—The Need to Get It Right 53

Your Record of Completed Assignments 58

Table of Contents

Part II—Why and How We Change

Introduction 59

Notes on Chapter 1...Changing My Thoughts
    ABC's of Changing My Thinking. 60
    Four Hurdles to Reoffending 61
    The Offending Cycle of Doom 62
    Lapse and Relapse 63

Notes on Chapter 2...Changing My Heart
    What Feelings?. 65
    Sexual Needs 67
    Sexual Fantasies 69
    Equality. 71
    Compatibility. 74

Notes on Chapter 3...Changing My Ways
    Intimacy Skills. 76
    Narcissistic Love Timeline 78
    Commitment 80
    The Abuse-free Lifestyle 82
    Fair Fighting 84
    Rules for Fair Fighting. 85
    Is This Relationship Working? 86

Further Reading and Related Films 89

Contact Information 90

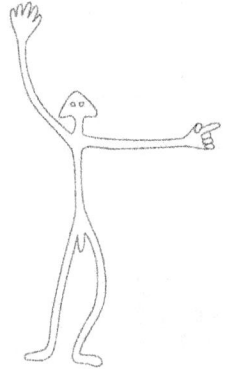

Introduction to Your Program

Few people are ever called upon to rebuild a life after taking such a heavy hit as you have taken. Of those asked to do so, many fall prey to despair, addiction, and suicide—some dramatically in one shot of a revolver, others on the installment plan through passivity or through substance abuse. Because of your commitment to the process of rebuilding your life despite an often overwhelming set of obstacles, you are heroic. You are heroic in facing a tremendous life challenge with courage, not only for your own sake, but for the sake of your family, your loved ones and those future souls yet to be touched by you.

You have enrolled in a unique program designed to help you reach more success than you may have ever thought possible. The back-story to our program and our emphasis on your success is what makes this program different.

Our back-story is in counterpoint to what you might experience in other programs. Other programs have a four point focus that stands in stark contrast to what you will experience with your program. The focus of some programs includes:

a shame-based approach that promotes never-ending, pathological amounts of shame about your past behavior

a heavy reliance on an avoidance/escape model of preventing future problems

an emphasis on repression of normal human longings and desires

a fixation on misbehavior

The program you are in couldn't be more different. Our approach to your treatment will be based upon four healing foundations:

respecting you, your gender and your sexuality

helping you learn to **manage your sexuality,** rather than being managed by it

encouraging you to **embrace normal human sexuality,** with its longings, thoughts, fantasies and diversity

establishing a **holistic base,** emphasizing success across the board in relationships, career and sexuality

We have every confidence that if you work the principles of the program carefully and honestly, you will experience success in your life beyond what you might ever have imagined. Through your work you will earn happiness, financial security, great friendships, a truly functional spirituality, and a wonderful love life—including a great sex life. Through the principles of the program you will achieve these goals honorably and legally, and they will be yours to keep.

You will work primarily in a group. Not everyone skips with joy when they find out they will be in a group. Group therapy is preferred for the kind of work you will be doing, but it is dependant on your honest participation and your respect of other people's comments.

Although you would never have wished your problems on anyone, your work on those problems will lead you to a new way of thinking. This new way of thinking will make possible a new life that will be better than you ever could imagine.

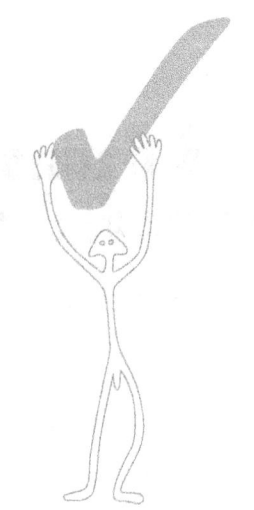

Program Orientation

This program exists due to many creative and provocative influences, among them: the twelve-step movement; Alfred Adler; Albert Ellis and Rational Emotive Therapy; Sigmund Freud (yeah, the one with the cigar and the couch) and a host of others too numerous to name. In effect, this program shamelessly borrows from anyone with good ideas. As we begin our work together there are just a few rules that we ask you to live with as we proceed:

- We show respect for others partly in our respect for their time. Thus, you must show up on time to group. You are allowed to come into group if you are up to 15 minutes tardy; however you will be required to perform 25 push-ups, 25 sit-ups, or read one poem aloud to group.

- If you are more than 15 minutes late you will not be allowed into group, but you will have to attend a one-half hour private make-up session that is billed at half the hourly rate.

- No one is successful in our society while maintaining disrespect for others. Thus, racist or sexist remarks are not tolerated in group. This includes the usual no-no's like name-calling, but also includes generalizations based on race or gender ("Women are just…" or "Men are all…" or "Whites/Blacks are all…"). Referring to yourself or to others in racist or sexist terms will not be tolerated and to promote this sort of respect, violators are required to give up ten push-ups for each infraction.

And that's it! Only three rules that are mostly about "playing well with others." Show up on time and don't put people down for the way they were born. Yeah, you also have to turn off your cell phone (10 push-ups) and pay for treatment.

Our Commitments to You

We have a consistent sense of awe and respect for our clients' courageous efforts to make comebacks from perhaps the biggest hit a person can take in this life. We know that you are dealing with a lot of problems right now. Some in the program are facing being labeled as felons for the rest of their lives, others are looking at losing marriages or contact with their children. All are dealing with the social stigma of being labeled as "sex offenders." **Our commitment is to treat you always with the respect you deserve for the courage you bring to making your comeback.** We could hardly teach you how to respect the rights of others by violating your rights in the name of "therapy."

Our focus is on three areas of success: *your career, your friendships, and your love life*. Our goal is to have you experiencing more success in each of these areas than you ever have in the past. Many have become cynical upon hearing this at first; but most have learned that these goals become a reality as they work the principles of the program into their lives. **We want you to be making more money than before and experiencing greater career satisfaction than you ever have. We want you to develop the best friendships of your life—people who really know you and accept you as you are and actually help you become a better person because of who they are. We want you to have more love (including the best sex of your life) as a result of your participation in the program.**

For this last to become true in your life our program promises to totally accept you as you are today, while at the same time challenging you and showing you how to change. The "change" part is really up to you, **but we will explain every detail of what you need to do to achieve success.**

We meet weekly with your supervising officers to help them better understand the work you are doing and to help us better understand what you are going through outside your time in group.

For Family and Loved Ones

You are already close to the one who owns this manual and you already care deeply or you wouldn't be bothering to read this. Please know that we deeply respect your loved one for his efforts to get his life back on track. In this program, his efforts are genuinely viewed as a heroic struggle.

The struggle part may be obvious—it's extremely hard for anyone in our society to make a comeback—so hard that one writer, F. Scott Fitzgerald, stated that there were "no second acts" in American life. Most of us have made some sort of comeback in life, from a failed career, a failed marriage, a life of drug abuse or perhaps all of these. But few of us have had to deal with a stigma as pervasive in our society as those labeled as sex offenders. No one, not drug addicts, not drug dealers, not even child murderers deal with the stigma of sex offenders—hence the word struggle. Coming back is definitely a struggle.

But "heroic?" Your loved one is heroic in the way that any hero is. A hero is someone who lays down his own personal life for the sake of others. A genuine hero may not be able to endure the thought of not laying down his life in certain circumstances—but despite his own personal interest in doing what he does, he is still also doing this for others. A hero does what he does to help others. He (or she) faces fear and adversity for the sake of a larger notion, that is, the love of those around him. Sometimes we call this love, "the greater good."

What can you do to help your loved one as they work their way through the program? First, read this manual. In doing so you will gather a sense of what is asked of participants in the program and the direction in which we are taking everyone. That direction is toward the goal of success—in all its forms. This includes relationship success (including a great sex life), financial success through career satisfaction; and lastly—deep, enduring friendships that will last through the hard times in all our futures.

Second, you can help by "keeping it real." After reading this manual (and with a great dose of courage) you will share a common vocabulary and you will be able to give and receive

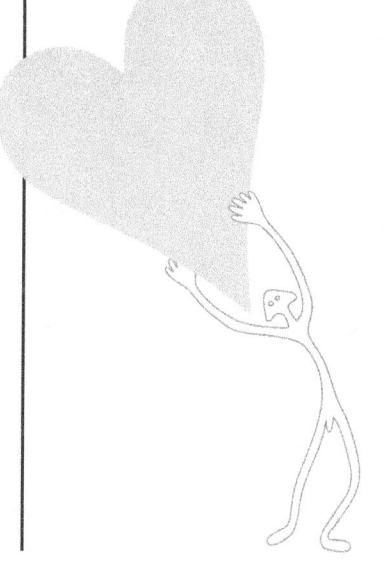

loving confrontation. Do not be afraid of confrontation—as long as it is abuse-free, confrontation (and even conflict) will help you and your loved one by establishing the truth as a foundation in your relationship.

Overview of Treatment Goals

Note: all written assignments have written directions that must be followed. Inform your therapist of which assignment you'd like to complete first and after receiving some feedback from your therapist, proceed. Show your therapist your assignment after doing some of it to make sure you're on the right track. After your therapist signs off on the assignments, make sure you keep them to prove later that you've done them if any questions may arise. Assignments can be typed (double space, one side), handwritten (if legible—as determined by therapist) or even audio taped if you are vision impaired.

Empathy & Respect

- Client will express genuine understanding of the harm that his personal victims and the victims of others have experienced, as demonstrated verbally in group.
- Client will express genuine remorse verbally and **in a written apology to victim.**

Success

- Client will complete either his high school education or obtain a GED.
- Client will work full time and *will ha*ve career goals as demonstrated by written career plan to pursue better jobs and more training. Retired clients will have a career plan that includes part time work or a program of lifelong learning or some other program of personal success.
- Client will demonstrate personal financial responsibility by opening an IRA or other retirement account, a checking account and by paying for treatment.

Social Skills

- Client will participate in abuse free relationships with both genders as measured by asking peers (male & female) out (to coffee, walks, working out, etc.) one time weekly. (See Practicum directions.)

- Client will engage in conflicts effectively and assertively, willingly, and in an abuse-free manner both in group and in personal life (role-playing personal conflicts in group).
- Client will engage in small talk appropriately while in relationship situations as measured by personal observations in and out of group in a public setting at least three times.

Cycle of Abuse

- Client will express cognitive understanding of his personal cycle of abuse by presentation to the group and in a collage (2' x 3') of pre-offense and current sexual thoughts and goals.
- Client will write an autobiography with an emphasis on how his lifestyle, choices, upbringing and so forth set him up for sexually acting out and what desensitized him to his behavior.

Relapse Prevention

- Client will verbally express responsibility for all behavior in group and out of group (apologies, confessions, restitution, etc.)
- Client will develop a personalized written plan of restitution to society in terms of compensation, charitable acts of good will, etc.
- Client will develop three coping strategies (with accompanying skills) for each stage of cycle of abuse as demonstrated in written plan.

Sexuality

- Client will demonstrate a healthy view of personal sexuality verbally and in written assignments based on B. Zilbergeld's book *The New Male Sexuality*.
- Client will demonstrate an appropriate knowledge base of human sexuality verbally and in written assignments based on the book *The New Male Sexuality*, by B. Zilbergeld.
- Client will engage in satisfying sexual activities of an honorable and legal nature as reported in group.

Cognitive Distortions

- Client will express verbally his understanding of the irrational beliefs that contributed to his criminal behavior and all of the above topics (relapse, sexuality, relationships, etc.) as demonstrated by his comments in group and his written log of personal irrational beliefs and the corresponding rational beliefs.
- Client will express cognitive understanding of his belief system dynamics in a group presentation at the board and in verbalized comments.

Spirituality

- Client will express his understanding of his personal defects and assets in a written spiritual inventory.
- Client will develop an adaptive spirituality integrating personal spiritual beliefs and personal sexuality as expressed verbally in group and by writing a paper describing his integration of spirituality and sexuality.
- Client will incorporate this adaptive spirituality into his daily life as expressed verbally in group.

How to Ruin Your Treatment

1. Avoid taking responsibility for your behavior: minimize, deny, or blame someone else. Minimize your behavior into such a miniscule subject that it's really not worth talking about. Deny your behavior so everyone will know you didn't do anything—so there's no need to talk about it. Blame others for your behavior ("she brought it on herself," or "my wife left me and that's why I…"). This will help you avoid looking at the past because the important thing everyone has to understand is that NONE of it is your fault.

2. Try if at all possible to pit your PO against your therapist. Put words in the mouth of one and then quote that imaginary line to the other. ("My PO told me I'm always going to have a curfew.") Complain about one to the other ("My counselor isn't any good, he just doesn't understand me.") This will take up important time that might otherwise help you or someone else as your counselor and your PO spin their wheels trying to get to the bottom of the nonsense.

3. Keep the focus on others in group—after all, they're all much sicker than you and need the time and the help more. Besides, you're pretty much over all the stuff that got your butt in trouble.

4. Fall in love. A time honored technique that has helped many avoid the messy painful business of growing up. You can fall in love with someone in your program, your therapist, your PO or perhaps if they are not cooperating, you may need to resort to one of the sick romantic patterns of your past—in any case the dawn of true love announces the arrival of the Good Feelings Fairy who will sprinkle good feelings on all that "getting healthy" nonsense.

5. DO NOT talk about your life. Do not open up to the group as this could ruin everything. If the therapist asks how you are, tell the group "I'm fine." Repeat this until even you believe it.

6. If you are not a drug abuser, start immediately. If you are a recovering addict/alcoholic—do not talk about your sobriety or lack of it in group—they might actually help you and then…what would happen to your denial? Sneak drinks and try to get someone from group to help you maintain the deception.

7. DENY, DENY, DENY that you are human, that you have a sexuality, that you have needs; never, ever take this therapy crap seriously.

8. Remember: Relapse is an impossibility.

8.
Remember:
Relapse is an impossibility.

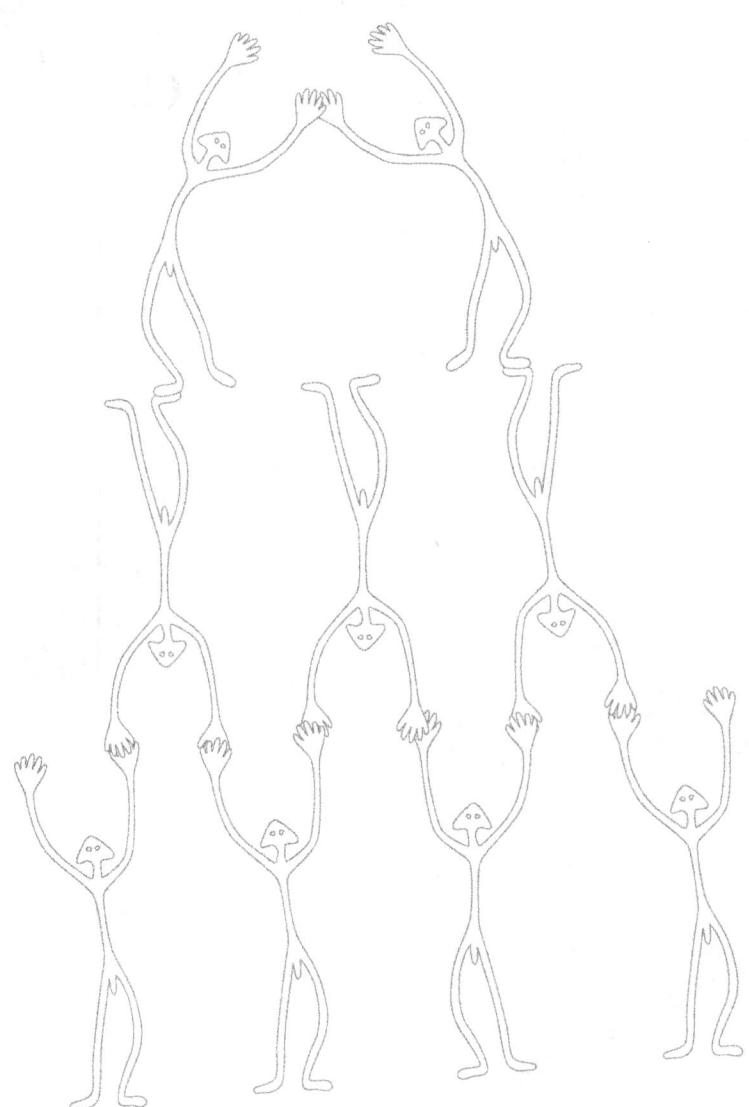

Part 1

Chapter 1:
The Need to Change My Thoughts

Accepting your present life as it currently exists is the first step toward change. If you do not like what has happened to you, you may be tempted to blame the legal system, or perhaps your parents, or maybe even God. This would be great because you can get mad at someone else and blame them. This would in turn lead you to thinking of yourself as the victim.

"I'm the only one here who's really been hurt, I didn't even have a victim!"

Or perhaps your victim "started the whole thing," or "she knew what she was getting into." So long as you are thinking of yourself as a victim you will never become capable of changing your situation. You will forever be a victim. You will continue to be a *re-actor* rather than an *actor*.

You probably already know you need to change. You likely already have the smarts, the guts and the overwhelming evidence to know that you and you alone are responsible for where you are today. What you don't know is what to do about it. This is where your program begins—showing you specifically what to you must do to turn things around and begin to change what's going on with your life.

All of us are a collection of our thoughts, our feelings, and our behaviors. Your program will help you to examine and change each of these three parts that make up you. Your program will help you become not what the rest of us think you should be, but more truly you, the genuine you, than you have been before.

The first chapter in Part I begins helping you by giving you the gift of knowledge. When you have completed Step 1 you will know far more about sex than most people.

> *"My best thinking got me where I am today."*

Step 1
The Need for Sexual Information

You are required to obtain a copy of Zilbergeld's New Male Sexuality. The book is available on-line, in the library, at all bookstores, or from people in group. For each chapter there are three questions that must be answered in writing. Turn in as many as two chapters in any week. Here are the questions you will answer for each chapter.

1. What did I read that I already knew?
2. What did I read that I didn't know?
3. What did I read that most related to my life?

"I've spent over twenty years in prison for two rapes. I'm fifty years old and living my life. I've been in therapy the last 14 years. I've been in this program the last year and a half. Takin' me a long time to get it right.

This program is different. We talk about everything. Everything is related to understanding your offense and why you committed it.

This is not going to be easy for it requires open-mindedness, honesty and abandonment of beliefs long held true. Give 'em up. You been to the joint and survived. Good for you. Keep the freedom and leave prison behind you. You ain't been to the joint? Don't go! Most of us thought about suicide at one time or another. Mention those feelings and deal with your depression. It's your choice though. Your responsibility. Take it and drive forward. There is an end to this. Work it and be done with it.

Shut the fuck up once in a while and be an old dog learning new tricks. In the "Shawshank Redemption," Morgan Freeman tells it like this, 'Get busy livin' or get busy dyin'.' Hope is there, but you gotta stand up and get yours   --J.Z.

Why am I doing this assignment / What's in it for me?

We need a group understanding, a common language, and a unified set of assumptions about male sexuality in order to effectively explore our individual sexualities in group discussions. When you have successfully completed this assignment you will have established an understanding of current knowledge about male sexuality as it is expressed across a wide spectrum. This text will give you an information base that we will use in group discussions to advance your treatment.

How does this assignment relate to my treatment / What's in it for me?

Answering the three questions involved in your written responses to each chapter of the book you will read for this assignment will give you a framework within which you will integrate the information in the book into your own life and your sexuality.

Finishing this assignment successfully will give you a knowledge base that you'll use in completing other assignments related to your treatment. You'll also use the information in the text to guide your responses in group discussions.

Since this assignment and its learning outcomes are so fundamental to your successful completion of your treatment, you should probably complete this assignment first out of the projects that are required of you during your time in the program.

How do I fulfill this assignment?

Obtain a copy of Bernie Zilbergeld's book, *The New Male Sexuality*. The book is available online through Amazon.com, at the local Borders Books, and at Barnes and Noble. Some copies may be available at a local branch of your public library.

Read each chapter carefully, even though you may already know about most of the information presented in each section of the book. Next, write or type your answers to each of these three questions on each chapter:

1. What did I read that I already knew?

2. What did I read that I didn't know?

3. What did I read that most related to my life?

Answer each question thoughtfully and completely, based upon your reading of the material in each chapter and your understanding or interpretations of the information presented.

ASSIGNMENT TITLE:
Responses to B. Zilbergeld Text
See page 14.

You may write about and submit questions relating to two chapters per week. A separate sheet containing your responses to each of the three questions listed above is required for each chapter.

What Does a Successful Assignment Look Like?

1. Your responses to each of the three questions on each chapter will be typed, neatly printed, or legibly hand written on a single sheet of paper. You'll produce one page per chapter, with your responses to the three basic questions for each chapter on every page.

2. Your answers to each of the three questions will show that you have carefully and thoughtfully read the chapter and have thought about your interpretations of the material in terms of your individual case, your needs, your sexuality, and your sex life.

3. No one word or one-sentence responses are acceptable. In your responses to the three questions on each chapter, you'll show that you've read the material carefully and that you have your own thoughts about and reactions to the information you've read. Please note that it's perfectly all right to disagree with some points that Zilbergeld makes in his book. The idea is that if you disagree, don't just say that he is out of line in his ideas. If you disagree with some idea in the book, phrase your own arguments carefully and demonstrate that your opposition to Zilbergeld's ideas is objective, logical, and founded in examples that you quote in your responses, or in your own experience, or in knowledge you've obtained from some reputable source. Be prepared to defend your own ideas in group discussions.

4. Be as specific and direct as you can be in your responses. Use complete sentences. Express your thoughts clearly and use appropriate language in your answers to each question. Your counselor may ask you about parts of your responses. Be prepared to discuss your ideas and the information you've read in group, in non-confrontational discussions.

How long will it take me to do this assignment?

There is no specific deadline for completion of this assignment. Once you have committed yourself to read the book thoughtfully, you may complete reading the text in whatever time frame you choose. Since you may submit your responses to only two chapters per week and there are 22 chapters, the entire project should take you at least eleven weeks to complete.

Step 2
The Need for Clear Thinking – Rational & Irrational Beliefs

This portion of your treatment is designed to help you by teaching you to discriminate between clear, logical thinking and irrational thinking. Irrational thinking supports not only criminal behavior, but all sorts of dysfunctional behavior. This dysfunctional behavior "seems so right" in the moment but never really helps us achieve our goals. If you wish to read more about this area of personal growth, look to works by Albert Ellis. Also, see the illustration on the *ABC's of Changing my Thinking* in "Information and Notes".

Your assignment is to list 25 irrational beliefs that you personally have bought into over the last decade or so of your life. Either alongside or below each of these irrational beliefs, you will write the corresponding rational belief. At least ten of the 25 must be about sex and romance.

Examples:

IB—If we're in love then we should be together.

RB—Being "in love" is only one of the necessary ingredients in a healthy relationship; more than just being in love is needed for success.

IB—I'll never be able to get ahead.

RB—No one but me is in control of my life; the only thing that's stopping me from achieving my goals may very well be me and my attitude.

ASSIGNMENT TITLE:
Rational and Irrational Beliefs
See page 17.

Why am I doing this assignment? / What's in it for me?

Our beliefs are a large part of who we are. Our beliefs form the basis of our personality, the way we present ourselves to the world, and the ways that we react to the actions of others.

Our beliefs may be rational or irrational. It's our irrational beliefs and our actions in following irrational or antisocial beliefs that can lead us astray.

When you have completed this assignment and discussed your ideas in group, you and your group mates and your counselor will better understand your beliefs, both rational and irrational. With understanding, you'll be better prepared to confront and rationalize dissonant ideas.

How does this assignment relate to my treatment?

This assignment relates to your treatment in that it helps you to confront irrational beliefs that may have helped lead you to your offense. Identifying and dealing with dissonant ideas will help you form attitudes and behaviors that conform to societal norms, thus helping your recovery.

How do I fulfill this assignment?

On two or three pages of legibly handwritten or neatly typed wording, you'll list at least 25 irrational beliefs and a corresponding rational belief for each item.

It may help you to divide each page of your response to this assignment into two columns; one for the irrational belief and one for the rational responses or alternatives to each irrational item. Here is an example, showing only the headings and one irrational belief and its more rational counterpart:

Irrational Belief:	Rational Understanding:
My penis is too small to satisfy a woman.	My penis is of average size and will satisfy a woman if I care for the person and engage in mutally acceptable activities.

What does a successful assignment look like?

You'll submit a typed, neatly printed, or legibly handwritten response to this assignment. Your finished assignment will be about three printed pages or perhaps two typed pages. You'll list an irrational belief, perhaps one or more that led you to your offense, and the corresponding rational beliefs. Your total list will explore *at least twenty-five* irrational beliefs and the corresponding more acceptable rational beliefs.

Note that *at least ten* of your irrational assumptions and the more accepted rational beliefs will relate directly to sexuality, romance, and interpersonal relationships. If you list more than ten beliefs related to sexuality, that's fine, but ten is a minimum.

As with other assignments you do for this program, you will be frank, explicit, and honest in revealing your beliefs. Your responses will be discussed in group meetings and you may expect full, non-judgmental discussions of your beliefs by your group mates and by your counselor.

How long will it take me to do this assignment?

You should allow at least two weeks to plan and think carefully about your assumptions with regard to your own sexuality and to your sexual relationships with other persons. Allow another week to carefully and logically phrase your ideas and write them out. A total of three weeks should be sufficient for this project.

Step 3

The Need to Embrace My Failure—
Just how did I get here?

Many of those who have been convicted of a sex crime find that they are confused about just how the whole matter came about. They often say that they have "no idea" how they came to commit their offense. To help with explaining that, most treatment programs help clients develop a "cycle of abuse" which involves a revolving wheel of one negative thing leading to another and then another until the offense occurs and then there's an attempt at covering matters up and then the cycle begins all over–again and again. The idea that sexual criminality is repetitive applies to many people–but not most convicted of sex crimes. Most of those who are guilty of sex crimes are not guilty of chronic criminal behavior nor do they typically engage in criminal thinking like a robber who is planning his next heist. Hardly any of those convicted of sex crimes have a clinically significant sexually deviant pattern of behavior. Some people just give up thinking altogether and assume that "sex offenders are different than normal people and they are just bad." This medieval way of thinking about why people do what they do is utterly unhelpful. It is unhelpful because it proposes that there are good people (who never commit such crimes) and bad people (the sort that do commit these offenses). With this approach, we can never predict behavior and that means we can never prevent such behavior because this approach is not a scientific one and it depends on what we can call the moral diagnosis. The problem is that we never can tell who's evil! Frankly, most people who commit sex crimes are pretty much like all the rest of us.

Many people either committed one offense and were caught or were in one sexually criminal relationship, as in one with a child incapable of legally giving consent, but these people have never behaved this way before. The vast majority of people who've committed sex crimes (over 90%) go on to never reoffend even without treatment. So, if only a small minority reoffend, why treat them all? Why treat them all as if they were career offenders?

These are good questions and the answers are too complex to be addressed here. Suffice it to say that the notion of a "cycle of abuse" is simply unhelpful to many because our lives are more complicated than what happened mere days or even hours before the sexual offense. The trajectory of our lives that led to the offense could have begun with the circumstances of our birth, our parents' treatment of us, and even the messages about sexuality that we internalized from our families, our religions or our society as a whole. The "cycle" is unhelpful in that it focuses on the short-term "causes" of criminal behavior rather than the big picture view of the many life variables that contributed to the poor decision-making that led to the crime. These are sometimes called *criminogenic variables* referring to the *crime's genesis* or beginning.

For just one example, consider someone born with Attention-Deficit/Hyperactivity Disorder. These individuals have a higher than average rate of physical, emotional and sexual abuse. They may struggle at school as a child. Their school troubles often lead to chronic disapproval from teachers and parents that, in turn, leads to discouragement, depression and anxiety. These emotions cause great stress in the lives of young people. Understandably, they crave acceptance and are often obtain it from other children who are struggling and perhaps smoking in a corner of the playground. This group provides acceptance, freedom from criticism and stress and often real understanding and camaraderie. They are also often able to provide greater access to the sorts of drugs that such children find comforting, like alcohol and marijuana. The young person's anxiety goes down and he feels better, while at the same time his grades get worse. Eventually, he either drops out of school or becomes antagonistic to academics. This leads to a poor education and often to chronic underemployment which leads, in turn, to a lifestyle unattractive to same-aged peers. However, younger girls may find this now older man's access to cars, cigarettes and alcohol attractive. With his adult male sex drive, these relationships are often sexualized and then he has sex with an underage girl and has a sex crime. Many offenders have such complicated stories but, once understood, the confusing pieces fall into place, and we can see how one criminogenic variable linked to the next, like a cascade of tumbling dominoes.

In this manual, we ask you to consider the criminal narrative in terms of your life's trajectory and to include all the criminogenic variables that led to your poor decision-making on the day you first committed your offense. Your assignment is to sketch out a meandering reverse S-curve that you can write on a piece of paper and then present it at the board in your group. Your counselor will help you. Think of this S-curve as starting at birth and ending at the time of your first (and perhaps only) offense. Note each variable: for example, "born with AD/HD," "started hating school," or "chose a mate who was abusive," and so on. Indicate the age at which these events began as you go along. Later, when you've completed this assignment with all your criminogenic variables and your attempts at self-soothing (like smoking pot), then your intervention plan for your life almost writes itself. You will find it especially helpful to think of this task as moving from the self-soothing behaviors of the past into self-care behaviors that help free and empower you. For example, I need treatment for AD/HD; I need to become more mindful about my career; I need to develop social skills so that I can begin to have meaningful friendships and later, intimacy skills so that I can have better relationships. This process takes time and courage, and you may need some help, but you will understand yourself better and have a clearer idea how to live the rest of your life. Ask questions of your counselor, be patient as you get to know yourself and your life's story from this healing point of view.

ASSIGNMENT TITLE:

How I Got Here

Why am I doing this assignment? What's in it for me?

People who commit sex crimes are mostly neither criminal in their thinking nor more deviant than anyone else in the general population. Even if you have a history of criminal thinking or a sexually deviant pattern of behavior–they too had their origins. Recognizing these origins and having a way to deal with each one of them will help you avoid additional crimes and obtain a more fulfilling life.

How does this assignment relate to my treatment?

Recognizing how my thinking and decision-making became impaired is critical to my recovery. This assignment will help you see the many contributors that led to the way of thinking that, in turn, led to the offense.

How do I fulfill this assignment?

You should save completing this assignment until you have done many of the other assignments and enough group work so that you have a real sense of the trajectory of your life. You can do the work in stages and fill in the blanks as time goes by every time you have new insight into yourself and your story. Ask your counselor to draw an example on the board and take notes as the counselor explains how one event or experience over time led to problems with your decision-making. After you have identified all of the major events and experiences of your life that contributed to your narrative, then take the time to briefly note what you're going to do, what you've already done or what you need to do to remedy the problem. Turn in your completed assignment to your counselor. Be prepared to discuss the stages in your narrative with your group members, in group. Expect fair, non-judgmental ideas from your group. Expect to revise and update your cycle as a result of group discussions and your counselor's input.

What does a successful assignment look like?

This assignment will take a page or so of typed, neatly printed, or legibly handwritten responses. Being honest and forthright is important but even more important is genuine understanding of your personal narrative leading to the crime. Respond thoughtfully to deal with and resolve issues in your life that contributed to your poor decision-making.

How long will it take me to do this assignment?

Allow yourself the luxury of completing many of the other assignments in this manual first. Then, begin making notes of the various influences that led to your decision(s) to commit the crime(s). Once you've got it all written down, show your work to your counselor, then your counselor will have you share your work at the board in group. It may take some time for you to complete the first draft. Your counselor may need a week to review it and your group will need one session.

Chapter 2:
Changing My Heart

Information is good, as far as it goes. We need information to make informed choices. Without the opportunity to make sure of my heart, I will always be prey to the doubts of myself and others.

For example, most individuals who have been labeled as a "sex offender" are sometimes stigmatizied or punished in any number of ways: employment, housing, friendship or even terminating a marriage over the matter. The offender often finds people labeling him as "evil," "dangerous," or "frightening." In the time following the offense many offenders become intensely depressed and, tragically, sometimes give in to the desire to "end it all." This pattern is the result of a number of thinking errors and over the time you are in the program these feelings and this outlook will change—at least for the offender.

As far as others go, consider this: some people are so upset by what you have done that they can no longer go on with you. Some folks are so upset by what people will think of them if they continue to associate with you that they cannot face this "guilt by association." But what would you have done? Would you be the sort of person who would dump others who'd done a similar misdeed? Would you reject your friend in his hour of need or your mate if she had been the one convicted of your crime? If your answer to these questions is "no," then perhaps you have been done a favor in this life. You have been disabused of the notion that you had something (a friendship, a love) that you really never had—at least to the degree that you presumed. Perhaps you can now go on to have much more meaningful, fulfilling relationships with people whose loyalty to you transcends the past.

This process starts with knowing your own heart. The steps that follow will help you better know yourself and what you stand for.

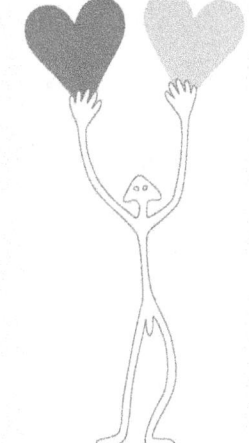

Step 4
The Need to Disclose — The Collage

We must know others and be known by them to avoid isolation and its bastard children, depression and lovelessness. Your work on this assignment will let others know you better; letting people "in" is essential to your healing. Virtually all offenders have led a life of isolation, and isolating oneself has become a difficult pattern to change. Even people who are socially very active often find that they failed to have real friends and genuine intimacy—the kind of friends and intimacy that would have enabled them to talk about their sexual feelings and thoughts long before they actually acted out in any way.

You must complete a collage that is about 3' x 2' in size. On one side you are to assemble drawings, photos, headlines from magazines, newspapers, your own work or even objects and glue them in such a manner that you are able to represent to others what was going on in your mind at the time of your offense (drug use, alcoholism, sexual fixation, guilt over family, workaholism, etc.) and on the other side you are to do the same with representing what is going on in your mind now. If there is no difference between the two sides, so be it. However, many people experience an extreme change between then and now and you should portray that as you are able. After arranging a presentation with your therapist, present your completed collage in group. Expect the group and your counselor to question you closely about your work.

Caution: If you try to present a collage that doesn't deal with your sexual thoughts and behaviors you will be directed to add these topics to your collage and make another presentation of your new collage to your group.

Why am I doing this assignment? / What's in it for me?

A collage is a pasted or glued presentation of images that relate to a central theme or idea. This assignment will help you in your treatment to better know yourself and let others in your group know about you better. You'll be more successful in your recovery when you allow yourself to reveal intimate parts of you to others in a non-judgmental atmosphere.

How does this assignment relate to my treatment?

This assignment relates to your treatment in that you will reveal parts of your inner self to your group mates. Revealing yourself and your thoughts relating to sexual matters helps others in your group to know you better and to talk with you candidly about your sexual thoughts and feelings as they relate to your recovery. Self-revelation in a welcoming, non-judgmental environment is a key part of your treatment and recovery.

How do I fulfill this assignment?

Get a piece of poster board about 2 feet by 3 feet in size. You may use the sort of poster board available at Walgreens, Target, or other store, or you may use a large piece of cardboard that measures about 2 by 3 feet. The color doesn't matter. You will use pictures, graphic elements, drawings, headlines from newspapers or magazines, or other graphic works from newspapers, magazines, and other sources to illustrate your sexual thoughts, as follows.

You'll glue or paste pictures, newspaper or magazine headlines, drawings, and other graphic elements on both sides of the 2 by 3 foot poster board. The graphic elements will represent significant parts of your sexual feelings, ideas, thoughts, conduct, or other parts of your sexuality before and after the offense that brought you to counseling.

One side of the poster board will represent your sexual thoughts and feelings before and leading up to your offense. The other side of the collage will represent your sexual thoughts and feelings in your post-offense and recovery period. Think of your collage as a "then and now" representation, or a "before and after" look at you and your sexuality.

Your counselor will show you successful examples if you have questions as to what images may go into this assignment.

What does a successful assignment look like?

Your collage is a very frank, candid visual presentation of your sexual thoughts, feelings, desires, conduct, and attitudes both before and after your offense.

ASSIGNMENT TITLE:
Produce a Collage
See page 24.

The basic idea here is that you will be very frank, candid and forthcoming in representing your ideas. Any picture, photograph, drawing, or graphic element is suitable as long as it relates somehow to your sexual ideas, thoughts, feelings, conduct, or desires both prior to and after your offense.

You will be prepared to present and candidly discuss the ideas and images shown in your collage at one of your group sessions. You may expect that discussions and reactions to your collage by your group mates will be very frank, candid, and forthright. While group members will be non-confrontational in their ideas about your collage, you may expect that your thinking will be challenged in honest and non-judgmental ways. Your group mates' comments will help you—and them—toward a more complete understanding of your motivations, your offense, and your current ideas about your sexuality.

The extent to which you are open, honest, frank, candid, and up-front about your pre-and post-offense ideas, thoughts, and feelings matters greatly in your presentation of your collage to your group members. Expect a full, fair, frank, and candid exchange of ideas about your presentation from your group mates.

Many people experience a significant change in their sexual ideas, attitudes, or opinions prior to and after the offense that gets them into counseling. Be prepared to present and discuss these ideas and to explore the changes you've gone through.

How long will it take me to do this assignment?
You should allow a couple of weeks to collect images that represent your thoughts and attitudes both before and after your offense. Allow another few days to assemble the images you select into some logical form for presentation. You should figure on about three weeks for completion of this project.

Tell your counselor when you are ready to present and discuss your collage. Your counselor will make time available during your regular group session for you to present your collage and for your group members to discuss your presentation.

Please don't assume that you'll be completely successful on your first try with this assignment. In discussions of your collage in group sessions, your group partners may make suggestions about what you have left out, what you have glossed over, or what is otherwise over or under-represented in your ideas either before or after your offense. You should be prepared to revise your collage to accommodate ideas presented by your group mates in discussions.

Step 5
The Need for a New Heart— Spiritual Inventory

All of us have been the object of "helpful" or "constructive" criticism—most of which was just nonsensical emotional abuse. You are the only human who really has a chance to know the inner you. Your assignment is to complete your spiritual inventory. This inventory is to include what you perceive as your character strengths as well as your character weaknesses. You are to list at least ten of each and to note three ways each of your items affects your life and the people around you. For example:

My Defect: I am frequently self-centered.

How this affects me: I am less successful in intimate relationships than I want to be.

How this affects others: People grow tired of my self-centered attitude and then avoid me, leaving me lonely.

My Asset: I am a creative man

How this affects me: My creativity brings me joy even when I am broke, unloved and disrespected.

How this affects others: People who understand and appreciate my creations find pleasure in them and want to experience more of what I have to offer.

Set up the above example in three columns: one for your defects (or assets), another for "How this affects me" and a third for "How this affects others."

As you share this in group, plan to have some fairly incisive feedback from others who may think you are being too hard on yourself (or too easy for that matter). The feedback you receive will be a "reality check" –but will not be hostile or critical.

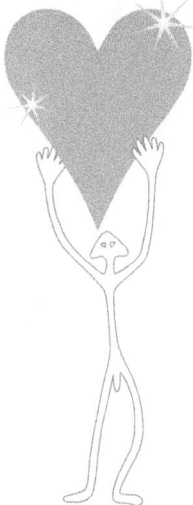

ASSIGNMENT TITLE: *Spiritual Inventory*

See page 27.

Why am I doing this assignment? / What's in it for me?

This assignment helps you know your inner self more completely. In knowing who you are and how your actions affect others, you are more likely to act toward others in constructive ways that enhance relationships. This will help you in your treatment and in your reintegration into society.

How does this assignment relate to my treatment?

Knowing yourself more completely helps improve your interactions with others and forging successful relationships with others. Being able to honestly confront your shortcomings and deal with them appropriately is a strong part of your recovery.

How do I fulfill this assignment?

List ten assets in your personal makeup or character and ten defects or challenges. For each asset or defect, write clearly and objectively about how the item affects you and how it influences others.

Be prepared to discuss your responses to this assignment in your group meetings. Expect that there will be insightful, non-confrontational comments from your group mates and from your counselor. Be prepared for frank, helpful ideas and candid, constructive comments.

What does a successful assignment look like?

You'll have about two pages or a bit more if your work is typed. You'll need four or more pages if your work is neatly printed or legibly handwritten.

Each page will be divided into three columns. In one column you'll list your asset. In the second column, you'll write about how this affects you. In the third column, you'll write about how your asset affects others. Here's an example of an "assets" page, showing only the headings and one asset:

My Asset:	How this affects me:	How this affects others:
I am a creative person.	Being creative brings me joy and helps me at work.	People appreciate my creativity and my different approaches to solving problems.

You will list a minimum of *ten assets* and *ten defects* in your character in your response to this assignment. Columns will be clearly labeled and content must be worded clearly and objectively.

If you choose, you may submit a preliminary draft of your response to this assignment to your counselor, or submit a few assets and a few defects to ensure that you're on the right track with your assignment.

How long will it take me to do this assignment?

Allow at least two weeks to plan and draft the list of your ten assets and your ten defects. Allow another week to discuss your assignment at a group meeting. Figure on taking about three weeks total for this project.

Step 6
The Need for Integrity— Integration of Spirituality AND Sexuality

If you were startled at seeing the words "sexuality" and "spirituality" in the same sentence and you are worried because you're not religious or because you don't want to be sacrilegious— don't be. You needn't worry because this assignment has nothing to do with religion; it does have a lot to do with spirituality. Wait, what? Well, one dictionary defines "spirituality" as that part of the human experience that deals with the unseen dimensions of our humanity. All humans have a set of beliefs about the unseen dimensions of our human experience but only some have a religion. What are some of the elements of the set of "All things spiritual?" Examples would include:

- What is the meaning of life?
- Why am I here?
- What is the true nature of love?

Some of the beliefs we've learned in this life have to do with our sexuality. Some of these beliefs are functional and some are not. Examples from both functional and dysfunctional include:

- My religion disapproves of masturbation.
- Any sexual expression between two unmarried people is wrong.
- My religion is more important that I am or than any other human being is.

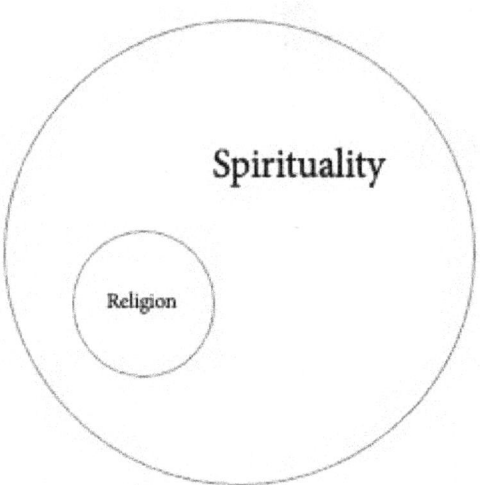

This assignment attempts to help you get to the core of your own personal spirituality by:

1 First, asking you to list your "Top 10 Spiritual Values." These might include items like: love, honor, integrity, compassion, and so on. It's your choice which of your many values you will list and you have no commitment to keep these values over time as they are simply a "snapshot" of your values on the day you do this assignment.

2 Second, please write one sentence that corresponds to each value and describes how you failed to allow this value to guide you in the time leading up to your crime. An example might include:

- "I failed to allow my value of compassion to guide me and instead exploited my victim as if they were not worthy of consideration."

3 Third, please write one sentence describing how you are allowing your own value (not your therapist's, not your PO's, not your wife's or anyone or anything else's values) to guide you nowadays. An example,

- "These days I ask myself if taking advantage of people and using them sexually conforms to who I really am and, if not, then I change my approach to a relationship or I let go of it and move on."

Doing this assignment will help you to understand yourself in the context of who you really are regardless of what others around you think. Doing this assignment will also help you understand your own true nature regardless of what anyone or any religion tells you what you should value. As a result of doing this assignment you will know yourself better and value yourself more as you go through life expressing your sexuality and your spirituality.

How do I fulfill this assignment?

You'll need to do some deep thinking on your own for this assignment. No matter what your spiritual path may be, your spiritual choices are going to govern your sexual activities—or maybe they won't.

There have been certain differences in the ways in which sexuality is perceived by religions since our human beginnings. Sometimes spirituality asks us to deny sexual drives and desires. Other spiritual paths embrace sexuality and acknowledge the primal nature of this human interest.

ASSIGNMENT TITLE:
Integration of Sexuality and Spirituality
See page 30.

Your finished response to this assignment will be six handwritten or printed or three typed pages. This stipulation as to length is intended to ensure that you will explore all the aspects listed on page 30 of the manual fully and honestly as they apply to you, your sexuality and your spirituality.

You will read your finished document in group. You'll discuss with your group mates your thoughts and how your own integration or your sexuality into your spirituality works or appears not to work.

What does a successful assignment look like?

You'll have at least three typed pages, or six or more legibly printed or handwritten pages.

Your document will be clear and honest. Any conflicts of what is preached by your religion and what is practiced by you in your sexuality will be clearly addressed and acknowledged in what you write.

You'll present your document, reading it aloud in a group meeting. Expect that you'll be asked about points that you write of that are not clear to your group mates. The questions will be focused on your ideas and will be non-judgmental and non-confrontational.

How long will it take me to do this assignment?

You should figure on at least a week to clearly and logically think through your ideas about your sexuality and how they relate to your spiritual path. Allow another week to draft, write, revise, and rewrite your document. A total of two or three weeks should be about right for this project.

Step 7
The Need for Compassion—Letter to Victim

In the course of writing your letter to your victim, please answer the following questions. Remember when writing, this is a letter that is never meant to be sent. It is a tool for helping you step away from the natural human defensiveness we all experience about acts of which we are deeply ashamed. Your work in completing this assignment will help you to allow your compassion to more fully develop to what would be normal for you.

1. How did your victim become your victim and not someone else?
2. What pleasure did you get out of what you did in your crime?
3. What do you feel most ashamed of in the way you treated your victim?
4. Explain how your irrational thinking held your victim responsible for what you did.
5. What was your fantasy about your crime prior to committing it?
6. How did your fantasy differ from what actually happened?
7. In the moment you abused your victim, how were you feeling?
8. How did you deal with your feelings during that time of your life?
9. What harm do you think you have done to your victim?
10. Can you imagine how your behavior has affected your victim?
11. What have you done to make amends for what you did to your victim?
12. How can you have any inner peace after what you did to your victim?
13. What makes you think you won't do something like this again?
14. What are you doing to make sure this doesn't happen again?

After writing your letter you will be expected to read it in group and you will be receiving feedback from the group and your counselor. Do not expect that process to be over quickly. Although the feedback will certainly be free of abuse, expect the feedback to be penetrating and confrontational.

ASSIGNMENT TITLE:
Letter to Your Victim
See page 33.

Why am I doing this assignment? / What's in it for me?

Understanding the harm done to the victim of your offense is a key part of your own recovery. Your ability to express your genuine human remorse and regret for harming your victim is a key part of demonstrating your own humanity. Part of your life after punishment is knowing that you have offended and being able to express that knowledge and your own regret.

How does this assignment relate to my treatment?

This assignment is a significant step along your road to recovery. When you can acknowledge that you've done wrong and offer a genuine regret and apology for your offense, you've come a long way toward becoming more fully human. A unique part of our shared human condition is that we can demonstrate shame for acts that we regret. This project will help you grow in your own humanity.

How do I fulfill this assignment?

Type, legibly handwrite, or print a letter to your victim. Note that this is a letter that you will absolutely *not* send, read, or otherwise show to your victim.

You will address *all* of the 14 points listed on page 33 of the manual.

You will submit a copy of your letter to your counselor, after you have read your letter aloud in group to your group mates. Expect that there will be some discussion about points made in your letter in group, after you've read the document.

In your letter, you will show an understanding of the affects that your offense had on your victim. You will also show compassion for the difficulties caused to your victim by your actions.

What does a successful assignment look like?

Your response to this project will be one or two typed, legibly handwritten, or printed pages. You will clearly and specifically address all of the fourteen points listed on page 33 of the manual.

You will demonstrate in your letter a depth and breadth of compassion and understanding appropriate to your offense. Your understanding of and compassion for the influences on your victim will be clearly shown in your letter.

You may clearly expect that you may go through a couple of preliminary drafts of your letter. You can't expect to fully and candidly explore all of the points listed on page 33 in your first attempt. Be honest and clear in the ways that you address each point in your letter.

How long will it take me to do this assignment?

Allow at least a week or so to draft, revise, rewrite, and clearly present your letter. You'll need to make an appointment with your counselor to set aside time during your group session to present your letter. Expect that this project will take at least three weeks to write and to present. If your counselor or your group mates find challenges or discrepancies in what you write, expect to spend additional weeks in revising and re-presenting your letter in group.

Chapter 3: Changing My Ways

If I get all kinds of new information about sexuality, and I understand what healthy sexuality and healthy living is all about but I don't change my behavior—then all my new thinking about sexuality and life is meaningless and sterile.

If I change my feelings about myself and about others, developing new insights and compassion for others, but I don't change my behavior—then my new feelings, insights, and compassion are only futile sentimentalism.

Changing my behavior is essential if I am to go on and have a successful life. My thinking has changed and my feelings have changed—but how do I actually do the new behavior that I want to do? Your program should coach you through these new behaviors. Your program wouldn't be much of a program if it didn't specifically show you what to do differently.

Your program doesn't practice "snap out of it" therapy. You know how that works, you get caught up in a self-defeating cycle of behavior and either you ask for help or someone observes what you're doing and then they say (you guessed it), "Snap out of it." Just as we *slowly* became who we were, we will *slowly* grow beyond that former way of living. Counseling can help speed the process.

Some of us need to wake up to the reality of life around us and your group will help you with that, but not knowing the specifics of *what to do* ensures defeat. Some of us who never allow ourselves to get angry need to begin expressing our anger assertively. Others of us who have been intimidating and abusive in our anger, need to perhaps go the opposite path. We all have our own path—but there is a need to know what to do.

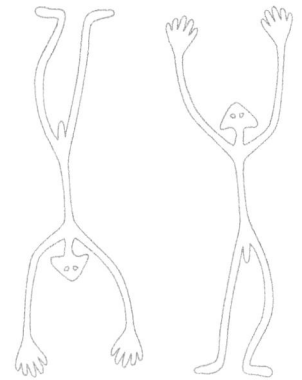

Some whose cycle has to do with the lack of sobriety must pursue sobriety and access the help of programs that work for them. Others have other specific problems. But *everyone's* cycle has to do with a lack of relationship success in his life. All sex offenders have used sex as a substitute for success in important areas of their lives.

This chapter and Step 8 through Step 12 of your program will help you turn this part of your life around.

Step 8
The Need for Friendship— Social Skills

All sex offenses occur within a context. Some elements of a given context could include substance abuse, depression, anger, or friendlessness. For many but not all offenders, learning to develop basic social skills would enable the offender to get many of his needs for love and acceptance met honorably and legally. Thus social skills competence is required of all participants in the program. To learn, to practice and to demonstrate this competence, participants are offered numerous opportunities in and out of group. The group process itself is an observation platform that enables your counselor to observe and sometimes to teach skills. These skills can also be learned by group participants from one another and should be applied not only to romances, but also to friendships and even to casual social contacts.

These skills include but are not limited to:

- initiating conversations and making small talk
- learning to be comfortable without needing to be "on"
- maintaining abuse-free relationships
- setting boundaries and defending those boundaries when needed
- terminating relationships when necessary without high drama

In addition to your work in group, you will be observed for 30 minutes three times in public by your counselor. Each of these occasions will be in a local retail establishment on the first Sunday of every month from 12:30pm to 2pm. You have the choice of which Sundays you would like to participate and you may change your mind at any time about showing up or not, since staff will be there regardless of whether any particular individual participates.

You can either bring someone or make the acquaintance of someone already there. The other party must be over 18 years of age and can be either a romantic interest or a friend, but not

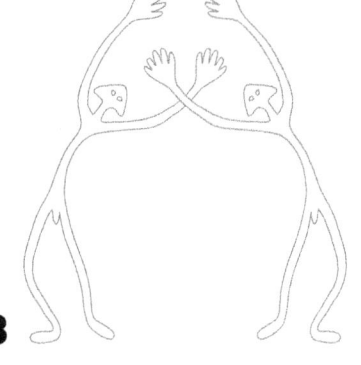

a relative. You must sit down in the café area with one other person for 30 minutes of conversation. Reading, staring off into space or similar disengaged behavior is unsatisfactory. Do not approach staff observing you. You will be timed; anything less than 30 minutes is inadequate. You are not required to buy anything and there is no additional charge for this part of your treatment.

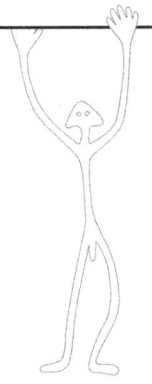

ASSIGNMENT TITLE:
Social Outings
See pages 38 & 39.

Why am I doing this assignment? / What's in it for me?

Social interactions on a person-to-person basis form the foundation of our human condition. This assignment will help you in your treatment to interact with one other person in a public setting for thirty minutes or more. Your success in this endeavor will help you to interact with people informally in social settings.

How does this assignment relate to my treatment?

This assignment relates to your treatment in that it helps you interact on an informal, interpersonal basis with other persons. Too many sex offenders feel marked by society as people who are not redeemable, rejected by or unworthy of participation in normal social settings. Completing this assignment marks part of your return to routine social interactions, in a public setting, observed by your counselor.

How do I fulfill this assignment?

The setting for your half-hour social interaction with another person is the coffee bar at a local site disclosed by your counselor. The basic idea is that you will bring another person to that place—or meet another person there—on the first Sunday of three separate months.

Your social encounter may be with a person of the opposite or the same sex. It's your choice. Your counselor will be in place from 12:30 to 1:30 p.m. on the first Sunday of every month to observe your presence and the presence of and evaluate your interaction with the person you bring with you or who you meet there. You will conduct social interaction / conversation with the person of your choice for at least one-half an hour, in the coffee bar seating area of Borders bookstore. Your counselor will carefully observe your interactions for the entire period.

It is not necessary that you acknowledge or greet your counselor; he will note and credit your presence.

You will attend three first Sundays in months of your choice. You may space out your visits as you like. Consecutive first-Sunday visits are not required. Be sure that you have your counselor sign in the appropriate place on page 58 of your manual after you've completed each visit.

What does a successful assignment look like?

You'll attend with a friend, acquaintance or another person for a minimum of one-half an hour on three first Sundays of three separate months. You may attend at any time between the hours of 12:30 and 1:30 p.m. Your attendance will be carefully noted and timed by your counselor, who will be observing discreetly.

You must bring (or meet) a different person for each of the three times. The idea of this assignment is that you'll meet with and interact with different sorts of people. If you want to "pick up" someone at Borders and interact with the individual for one-half hour, that's fine.

You'll stay with the person you bring or meet, engaging in conversation for at least one-half hour. The important part of fulfilling this assignment is that you engage in normal, routine, non-sexual, social interaction with another person. Anything less than one-half an hour will earn you no credit for that Sunday. If you choose to stay for more than one-half an hour, that's up to you.

Do not attempt to contact your counselor during your time at Borders. Your presence, the fact that you have brought another person, and that you interact with that person for the required half hour will be carefully noted.

How long will it take me to do this assignment?

It will take you three first-Sundays to complete this project. You'll spend at least one-half an hour on three Sundays interacting with one other person. You'll take three months to complete this stage of your treatment.

Step 9
The Need to Make Things Right—
Plan of Restitution

As recently as the 1960s there was a phrase current in our language that went something like, "he's paid his debt to society." The phrase was used in movies and in common speech in sentences like, "Yeah he did a bad thing, but he's paid his debt to society." The idea was that somehow, even though I committed an anti-social act in my past, I could set matters right by paying restitution, paying a fine or serving some time in an institution and so forth. This mechanism in our society allowed one to get a fresh start, because all debts that could be paid were paid in full.

In our current culture there is no such mechanism, especially for sex offenders. No combination of many years of incarceration, parole, probation, fines or restitution payments seems to be enough to escape the stigma of being labeled "sex offender." Both for offenders and for society this is unfortunate in the sense that there is no finish line in sight, no goal that once achieved, brings an end to this stage of our lives. In light of this development one might wonder why and how a "Plan of Restitution" could fit into any current treatment program.

That answer is contained in each one of us; we all know we want to be able to say, "Although some wrongs can never be undone, I did what I could to make that right." Such a response allows us to take responsibility for our actions and makes a way for respect to exist.

How does one make such a matter right? There are a number of creative ways to address the problem using a combination of good works dedicated to your victim involving sacrifices of time, money or talent. Your assignment is to formulate a plan which allows you to say to others and yourself, "I've done what I could to make matters right." You are encouraged to consult with your therapist and with the group so that you neither overdo your restitution nor avoid your responsibility.

> "If you believe in God by any name, ask for his forgiveness and know he will forgive you if you are sincere. Then, go and do not repeat your illegal act which brought you to this point, but look inside yourself—not to your friends, family or mentor of any kind—for the strength to overcome. Do not be afraid if others are suspicious; as long as you know you are doing right your inner peace will remain. Finally, have or develop your sense of humor when it comes to sex."
>
> D.R.

Why am I doing this assignment? / What's in it for me?

Making amends for a crime committed in a society is fairly straightforward for most offenders. They are apprehended, tried, convicted, and they serve a fixed term in prison. They pay a fine, do community service, or otherwise repay society for their crimes.

This is not the case for sex offenders. When one is convicted of a sex crime, he or she is marked figuratively at least with the mark of the beast and excluded from further redemption or participation in normal society. Opposing and overcoming this common wisdom on the part of society at large is a key portion of your reintegration into the society in which we all live and work.

Living honorably and successfully in our culture is probably the best way to contradict the routine assumption that a sex offender can never be rehabilitated. This assignment helps you develop ways to live honorably and well, in personal contravention of the idea that sex offenders can never be effectively rehabilitated into American society.

How does this assignment relate to my treatment?

Your treatment in this program seeks to integrate you and your honorable sexuality into the mainstream of our culture. This assignment will help you to acknowledge your offense, its seriousness and affects, and to strive beyond your failings toward a more honorable, acceptable, and effective participation in American society.

How do I fulfill this assignment?

This assignment makes you look deeply within yourself and your motivations: the motivations that you have to redeem yourself in the eyes of your higher power, your significant others, and (as far as possible) in the understandings of the culture in which you live.

Think about the offense that brought you to the point where you are today. How will you make amends for your offense? To whom will you make amends? How will you prove to society and to yourself your own continuing worth and your suitability for both forgiveness for your offense and for reintegration into the society of people in which you aspire to function honorably?

Your understanding of these questions and your responses to these points will form the basis of a short document that proposes a plan for restitution that will comprise a key part of your recovery.

What does a successful assignment look like?

Your plan of restitution will amount to about two typed pages

> **ASSIGNMENT TITLE:**
> *Plan of Restitution*
> See page 42.

or four or slightly more neatly printed or legibly handwritten pages. Here is an outline of the minimum points that you will consider in your plan of restitution:

Your Name:

Plan of Restitution:

I accept:
- The fact that I have committed an offense by...
- The idea that I am responsible for...
- The concept that I have made choices that...

I know that:
- I have done wrong by...
- I must make amends for...

To avoid reoffending, I am determined to:
- 1.
- 2.
- 3.

My thinking was wrong prior to / during my offense in that:
- 1.
- 2.
- 3.

To assuage the guilt I feel for committing the offense of which I am convicted, I will:
- 1. Seek the forgiveness of my higher power
- 2.
- 3.

To make restitution to my victim and to society for the offense of which I stand convicted, I will:
- 1.
- 2.
- 3.

Please note that this is only an outline. Include *all* of the points addressed in the outline, and also include any other ideas that you see as relevant to your individual case or to your life and the circumstances of your offense.

Also note that this plan of restitution will never be shown to your victim. The document is purely for use in your treatment, and will never be shown to anyone related to your offense in any way whatsoever. Your counselor will review the document you submit. Your group mates will discuss your ideas and will give you honest, candid feedback about the contents of your document.

Please note that this is only an outline of minimum contents for your plan of restitution. You may very well see the need to include additional elements or other information about how you plan to make amends for your offense. If you leave something out or include ideas that are not relevant, your counselor and your group mates will let you know. Note also that you will *not* show your plan to anyone but your counselor and your group mates.

You will present your plan of restitution in a regular group meeting. Your group mates' comments on your plan will be focused, relevant, and insightful. You may be asked to revise and re-present your plan as needed.

How long will it take me to do this assignment?

This project should take about a week for you to carefully think about your offense, the consequences of your offense for your victim, and the affects on your victim and on society. After planning and thinking, allow another week to write and revise your ideas about making restitution for your offense within the framework of the outline given. Figure on spending at least two weeks to develop, write, edit, and re-write your response to this assignment. Revisions and rewrites may make this a more lengthy and involved project. When you have questions or concerns, contact your counselor.

You will present this document to your group mates in a routine group session. Expect that your group mates will have some candid, non-confrontational ideas about what you write. Be prepared to discuss and defend your ideas in a non-judgmental environment. Be prepared to re-write and revise some or all of what you write as a result of ideas you obtain in group discussions.

Step 10
The Need to Understand the Past — Autobiography Assignment

One of the more difficult assignments that you must complete to graduate from the program is the autobiography. Its completion will help in successfully achieving a level of awareness that can allow one to "have sexuality" rather than letting your sexuality "have you."

The difference is one of perspective, the result of some reflection and then sharing that reflection with others. Plan on discussing in group your completed 30-page or longer autobiography after your counselor has had a chance to read it. The autobiography should address the barest outlines of your life, but pay strong, careful attention to your sexual development. Topics you should address include:

- How you learned about sex as a child
- Your sexual memories as a child
- Any history of sexual abuse
- Personal history of sexual play with others (spin-the-bottle, etc.)
- Your knowledge of your parents' sex lives
- Your religious training (if any) regarding sexuality
- How you discovered masturbation, your feelings about masturbation, and what you thought of when masturbating as a youngster, did anyone walk in on you?
- Your first sexual experience with another person
- Sexual experiences with same sex and opposite sex partners
- Experiences with deviant sexual behavior (peeping, exposing, fetishes, attraction to children, etc.)
- Your beliefs at the time of any deviant or criminal sexual behavior

> *"Those who do not understand the past are condemned to repeat it."*
> — Santayana

- Your history of noncriminal sexual acting out (e.g., affairs, sexual harassment at work, etc.)
- Your current feelings about masturbation and your masturbatory fantasies
- Your current sex life, who initiates, how often, is it mutually satisfying
- Can you talk about sex with your partner(s); do you know their history, fantasies, and thoughts during sex; do you understand and accept their private sexual experiences?
- Your current religious beliefs, how you got them and how they affect your current spirituality's interaction with your sexuality.

ASSIGNMENT TITLE:
Your Autobiography
See pages 46 & 47.

Why am I doing this assignment / What's in it for me?

The great Greek philosopher Socrates once said, "The unexamined life is not worth living." This assignment will help you and your counselor understand your life so far and identify significant aspects of your development as a person and as a sexual being in today's world.

How does this assignment relate to my treatment?

This is one of the more challenging assignments that you must complete to graduate from your program of counseling.

Finishing this assignment successfully will give you a broad perspective on your life. From this perspective you will help yourself gain insights into the "why" of the offense that brought you to counseling.

Looking back and considering your life from the perspective of today is a uniquely satisfying and changing experience. The insights you gain from thinking clearly and logically about your life thus far will help you in forging ahead successfully into what you make of your future.

How do I fulfill this assignment?

This assignment requires that you will carefully, candidly, and honestly look at your life thus far. You will write with significant details about all of the points listed on pages 28 and 29 of the manual. Merely addressing or answering the points listed is not sufficient. You will weave your responses to the items listed into a coherent narrative that tells the details of your life thus far. Carefully and completely tell a reader of your life thus far. Honest confrontation of the events of your life, even the unpleasant events, is a prime requirement of your autobiography.

Write clearly and do not avoid any of the issues listed in the manual. Be candid and honestly tell about the events that brought you to the place you are today. Write objectively, without seeking sympathy or condemnation from a reader. Provide details about your life events. Tell honestly about the affects on you as a person, upon your development, and upon others (parents, siblings, wives, lovers, etc.) in your life. Tell a reader of the outcomes of the events of your life. Show a reader clearly the importance (the "so what?"), of the events you tell about.

Please don't expect that your first draft of your autobiography will be sufficient to fulfill this assignment. Be ready to revise and rewrite pages, sections, or your entire document in order to provide details, tell of outcomes, explain circumstances, or otherwise make the events of your life and their significance plain to a reader.

It's probably a good idea to let your counselor read a preliminary draft of your early efforts for writing for this project in order to be certain you're on the right track. Help in structuring your writing is available at a modest charge if you need it. Talk to your counselor.

Be ready to discuss some significant details of your finished autobiography with your counselor and with your group mates.

What Does a Successful Assignment Look Like?

1. Be as specific, comprehensive, detailed, and direct as you can be in writing of your childhood and your life thus far as an adult. Use significant details of your early development, of your family life, and of your coming of age as a sexual being, involved in living successfully in our culture.

2. Your autobiography must be a comprehensive exploration of all of the bulleted points listed on pages 46 and 47 of the manual. An acceptable autobiography must address all of the points listed and will incorporate the points listed into the narrative flow of a complete story of your life thus far.

3. Be detailed, candid, and honest in your careful exploration and narration of all aspects of your sexual development. You are reflecting here on your early development, your adolescence, and your adult life thus far. Be certain that you do not "short change" any of the points listed on pages 46 and 47.

4. Your finished autobiography will be typed or legibly printed or handwritten. Since this is a careful, honest, complete and detailed story of you, the finished document will be a *minimum* of 30 pages typed, or significantly greater length if legibly handwritten or printed. This minimum length is specified in order to ensure that you will include sufficient detail and clarity in a comprehensive examination of your life.

5. Your counselor will read your autobiography carefully. Expect that you will have to make some revisions to enhance details or further explain some aspects of your life story.

How long will it take me to do this assignment?

In examining your life carefully and completely, you'll naturally take a good length of time. Clearly order the events of your life thus far. Write of the events clearly. Make the significance of the events you tell about meaningful to a reader—as meaningful and significant to a reader as they are to you. You'll take at least three months to write of your life in a successful autobiography; perhaps a bit longer.

Step 11
The Need for Success— Career Plan

So often, those who have committed a sex offense can look back and see that they have used sex as a substitute for success. Building a career is vital to long term recovery and a profound sense of success. Your career is much more than you current job. Your career is your life's work. Your life's work may involve temporarily working in an unpleasant situation to achieve your long term goals. Indeed, this is the essence of the maturity needed for success—the ability to defer gratification.

Your assignment is to think about who you are and what you want out of your life. You may consult professionals or your group as needed to develop a written career plan. Your career plan will likely need only one page to lay it out to your group and your counselor. Feel free to read articles and books for additional information. All community colleges employ people who specialize in this area and who are available free of charge or at an extremely nominal fee.

Retirees in the program must also write out a career plan because our work is part of what defines us in our lives. Certainly, we are more than our jobs. We (hopefully) have a rich life aside from and often in contrast to our professions. Yet, our work provides goals that feel great to achieve and the means to achieve other personal goals like caring for those we love. In retirement we can continue to love those we care about (including ourselves) through our work. Being retired can liberate one to pursue the life path found to be most gratifying and meaningful. Consider writing, volunteering time, mentoring others and so forth. A lifelong plan of learning, growing, and travel has been embraced by some retirees and their career plans included specific travel goals, learning new skills like ballroom dance, getting a garden growing and so forth.

The first paragraph of your Career Plan should be your Mission Statement. Those paragraphs following the first will describe how you intend to fulfill that mission. Your Mission Statement is a one-sentence summary of why you are here on this planet. What are you doing with your life? Why do you occupy your space in this universe? Where is your meaning found?

Why am I doing this assignment / What's in it for me?

Having a clear idea of what you want to do and how you will accomplish what you've decided to do helps you focus your energies and attention on just how to achieve the goals you have set for your life and work.

You'll be more successful in your recovery and in your life as an adult when you have some clear, reasonable ideas about where you're going and how you're going to get there. A clear plan for your career and an explicit contract that tells how you'll achieve success will both help you to focus your energies and to enhance your progress toward reintegration into society and success in your chosen career path.

How does this assignment relate to my treatment?

Aristotle wrote that "We are what we repeatedly do. Excellence, then, is not an act but a habit." Your work is an essential part of who you are. Real success in life rarely is the result of luck. Rather, a logical career plan helps guide our efforts in the world of work and helps us along a planned career path toward success in a chosen endeavor.

Long term success is closely linked with long term satisfaction in life. This assignment relates to your treatment in that it helps you focus your efforts on those things that most clearly help you toward your career goals. When you are working toward explicit goals, your activities are more rational, more focused, and more effective.

How do I fulfill this assignment?

Carefully read the information in the manual on pages 50 and 51. A successful career plan will address the following points as a minimum:

1. Clearly identify the career you've chosen. Give it a title.

2. Demonstrate to a reader exactly where you stand now in your progress toward success in your chosen career field.

3. List the educational requirements for further success in the career you've identified.

4. Explain how you will fulfill the educational requirements to enhance your career plan.

5. Give specific details of the sorts of work you'll engage in during your career in whatever field you've chosen. Make the details of a typical day at work in your chosen career clear to a reader.

ASSIGNMENT TITLE:
Career Plan
See page 50.

6. Show a reader clearly just why this sort of work interests you and why the work is meaningful / fulfilling to you. It has to be more than just a job if you're planning a career in the field you've chosen.

7. What is a realistic expected annual income for a person in the career field you've chosen? Give reasonable figures for both people at the entry level and at the top level incomes for positions in the career field you've selected.

8. Make a mission statement the first paragraph on the first page of your career plan. A mission statement is a one or two sentence explanation of exactly what you plan to do or to achieve (what your "mission" is), and a general overview of how you'll achieve or fulfill your mission. Here's an example of a mission statement: "I will achieve success as a precision machine tool maker by developing and extending my abilities through education in TMCC's Precision Toolmaking Program. I will further develop my skills through work and extensive training until I achieve the status of Master Tool Maker."

This mission statement tells a reader about what your goal is (" . . . achieve success as a precision machine tool maker . . ." The other part of the mission statement tells about the means toward that goal. The ultimate goal or outcome is shown (" . . . achieve the status of Master Tool Maker.").

What does a successful assignment look like?

You will have at least one and a half typed pages for your career plan. You'll have slightly more than two pages if your career plan is either neatly printed or legibly handwritten.

For your success contract, simply fill in the blanks on the pages provided. It may help you to photocopy pages 54 and 55 of the manual to complete your rough draft of your success contract. Then consult with your counselor, your spouse or partner, or with others in your life to ensure that what you put into your contract is attainable or "do-able."

How long will it take me to do this assignment?

Allow at least a week or perhaps a bit more to research the requirements for your career path. Consult with your significant other and with your counselor for help in preparing your success contract (pages 54 and 55 of the manual). The two parts of this assignment should take you about three weeks to accomplish successfully.

Step 12
The Need to Get It Right— Contracting for Success

After a history of hurting others and in dealing with one's own wounds, no one can afford the luxury of going through it all over again. We will have slips certainly and we could most assuredly get caught up in a self-defeating cycle of neediness and the misbehavior that follows not addressing our needs—but we cannot reoffend, the consequences to ourselves are too great, the hurt caused to others is too heavy a burden to bear.

The following assignment is designed to help you in getting it right. Getting it right means you will make mistakes, but not fatal ones. You will have pain, but not misery; failures, but you will not have a failed life.

Feel free to make another personal copy for your partner or spouse. Everyone on your team needs to know what to look for and what to do about the problems that certainly will arise in the future.

Don't hurry and fill out the following pages until you have made notes and consulted with your group and therapist. Take your time and get it right. When you're done, give your therapist and your PO a photocopy of the finished copy.

Success Contract (Rough Draft)

Name:_____

This contract helps me to maintain my success by identifying risk factors that indicate that I am at higher risk and figuring out what I can do to help myself stay safe.

Warning Signs

High-risk situations I must avoid:

1._____

2._____

3._____

How I act out or overreact to others:

1._____

2._____

3._____

Feelings that indicate that I am not doing so well and that I might need some help:

1._____

2._____

3._____

Negative ways of thinking, seemingly unimportant decisions, irrational beliefs, cognitive distortions, etc. **(particularly about sex!)** that indicate my thinking is not what it should be.

1._____

2._____

3._____

Behavior that shows I need to take action. This may include high risk behavior that anyone could see (taking drugs) or seemingly normal behavior that is part of my unique cycle.

1._____

2._____

3._____

Alternatives: If I find risk factors in my life, I will..

1._____

2._____

3._____

4._____

Signature: _____

Therapist's Signature: _____

Success Contract (Finished copy)

Name:_____

This contract helps me to maintain my success by identifying risk factors that indicate that I am at higher risk and figuring out what I can do to help myself stay safe.

Warning Signs

High-risk situations I must avoid:

1._____

2._____

3._____

How I act out or overreact to others:

1._____

2._____

3._____

Feelings that indicate that I am not doing so well and that I might need some help:

1._____

2._____

3._____

Negative ways of thinking, seemingly unimportant decisions, irrational beliefs, cognitive distortions, etc. **(particularly about sex!)** that indicate my thinking is not what it should be.

1._____

2._____

3._____

Behavior that shows I need to take action. This may include high risk behavior that anyone could see (taking drugs) or seemingly normal behavior that is part of my unique cycle.

1._____

2._____

3._____

Alternatives: If I find risk factors in my life, I will..

1._____

2._____

3._____

4._____

Signature: _____

Therapist's Signature: _____

Completed Assignments

(Please check with your counselor for which assignment to do next.)

Step 1 (The Book) Date: _____ Counselor's signature: _____

Step 2 (Irrational Beliefs) Date: _____ Counselor's signature: _____

Step 3 (How'd I get here?) Date: _____ Counselor's signature: _____

Step 4 (Collage) Date: _____ Counselor's signature: _____

Step 5 (Spiritual Inventory) Date: _____ Counselor's signature: _____

Step 6 (Spiritual Integration) Date: _____ Counselor's signature: _____

Step 7 (Victim Letter) Date: _____ Counselor's signature: _____

Step 8 (Social Outings) Date: _____ Counselor's signature: _____

                       Date: _____ Counselor's signature: _____

                       Date: _____ Counselor's signature: _____

Step 9 (Restitution) Date: _____ Counselor's signature: _____

Step 10 (Autobiography) Date: _____ Counselor's signature: _____

Step 11 (Career Plan) Date: _____ Counselor's signature: _____

Step 12 (Success Contract) Date: _____ Counselor's signature: _____

Why & How We Change

Introduction

Part II

The following notes and illustrations are offered as background reading to provide supplemental information. They are based on the teaching part of your group experience. They correspond (imperfectly) to the Steps in Part I.

Among the most unhelpful suggestions in the world are those inane one-liners that are perhaps meant well sometimes, but are usually steeped in shame. Among them:

"Grow up!"

"Snap out of it!"

"That just isn't appropriate."

The last example is especially modern in that it replaced our shaming notions formerly referred to by such words as "naughty," "bad," or "sin." Even some counselors fall into this usage of these words.

The truth is, we would all do better if we knew better. Oh sure, we know that certain acts are wrong—the problem often is that we simply don't know what else to do. We don't know any better way of living and of getting our needs met. The information that follows is an attempt to explain the calculus of human relationships in a logical, straightforward manner that will appeal to thinking human beings. If you are one of these, rejoice! If not, then,

Snap out of it!

A lot of what follows isn't just for people with a history of sexual criminality—it's for everyone who wants to have successful relationships and happy families. So much of sex offending grows out of isolation, poor relationship skills, social skill deficits and other matters having nothing directly to do with criminality. All of the following has been tested by lots of people—and it works.

ABCs of Changing My Thinking

Albert Ellis, borrowing from ancient Stoic philosophers, identified a way of looking at life that seems to focus our power in an extremely effective way. In a nutshell, he stated that we were unable, in this vale of tears, to change our *feelings* or the *events* that seemed to cause our feelings to change from one to another. My mother dies, my mate loves me, my dog bit the mailman, the stock market crashed—all of these events could seem to make me sad or happy or mad or some other feeling. What Ellis did was point out that there was an intermediary between our feelings and the events that seemed to control them. He stated that we had a **belief system**. This belief system, unlike the other two components, was under our control. We could examine these beliefs and, if they were nuttier than a fruitcake, exchange them for more rational beliefs. Better still, we had control over this process. If you've ever been to a 12-step group they refer to the irrational beliefs that cause us so much trouble as "stinkin' thinkin'." The following schematic illustrates Ellis' idea.

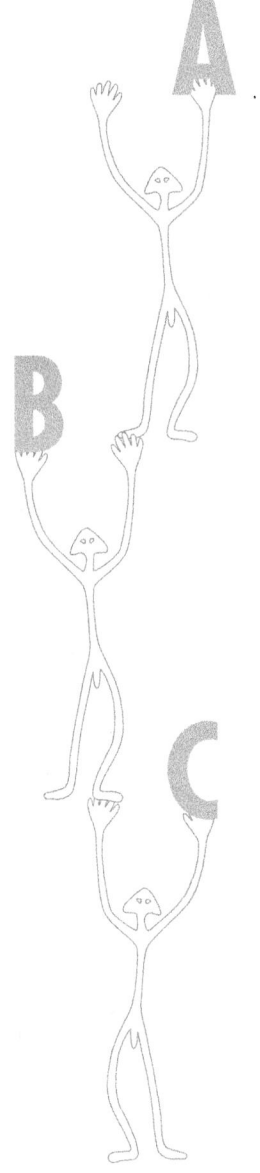

Activating Events
↓
Belief System
↓
Emotional **C**onsequences (or feelings)

Four Hurdles to Reoffending

Although few offenders ever plan to reoffend, relapses do occur. In order to reoffend I have to overcome four obstacles before I can commit another sex offense.

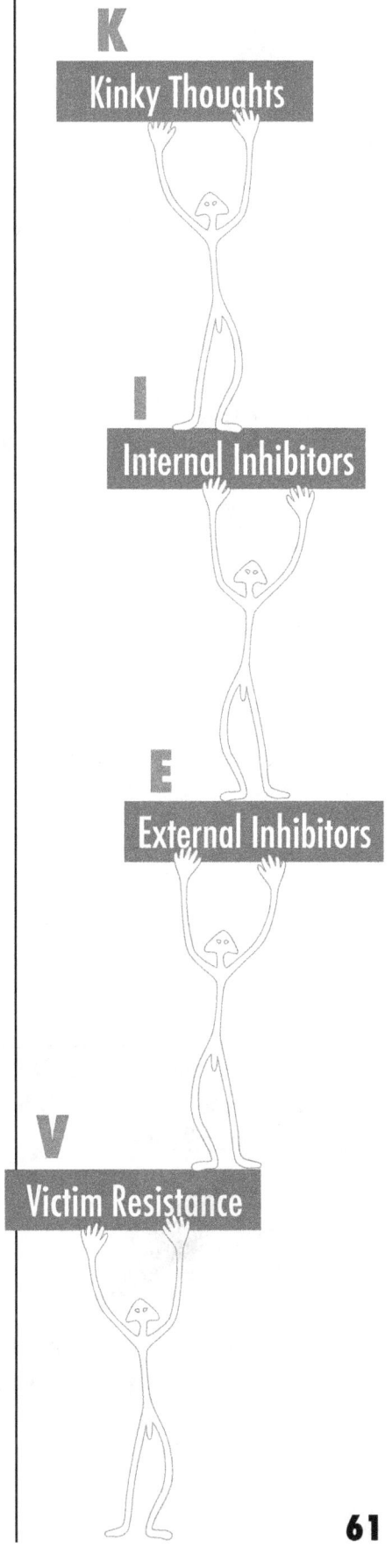

1. I have to develop socially or sexually deviant ("**kinky**") thoughts to an adequate extent before I can act on them. Such thoughts always precede illegal behavior.

2. I have to overcome the **internal inhibitors** that would normally keep me from reoffending. These would include the fear of the consequences of my acts, my normal guilt about hurting people, my empathy for the suffering of others.

3. I have to then overcome the **external inhibitors** that prevent my committing the offense. These would include overcoming the suspicions of others, the physical obstacles like locked doors, and avoiding police intervention.

4. Lastly I must overcome any **victim resistance**. This can be achieved through grooming, physical assault, blackmail, and so forth.

If I understand that I must overcome these hurdles before I can commit another offense then I can forestall another offense by being aware of my behavior. This knowledge is one more tool that would arrest my cycle of abuse. To make it easy to remember, think of the word "KIEV." Kiev is the capital of the Ukraine and Chicken Kiev is a delicious dish. Yeah, whatever—it's just a suggestion. KIEV. **K**inky thoughts, **I**nternal inhibitors, **E**xternal inhibitors and **V**ictim resistance.

The Offending Cycle of Doom

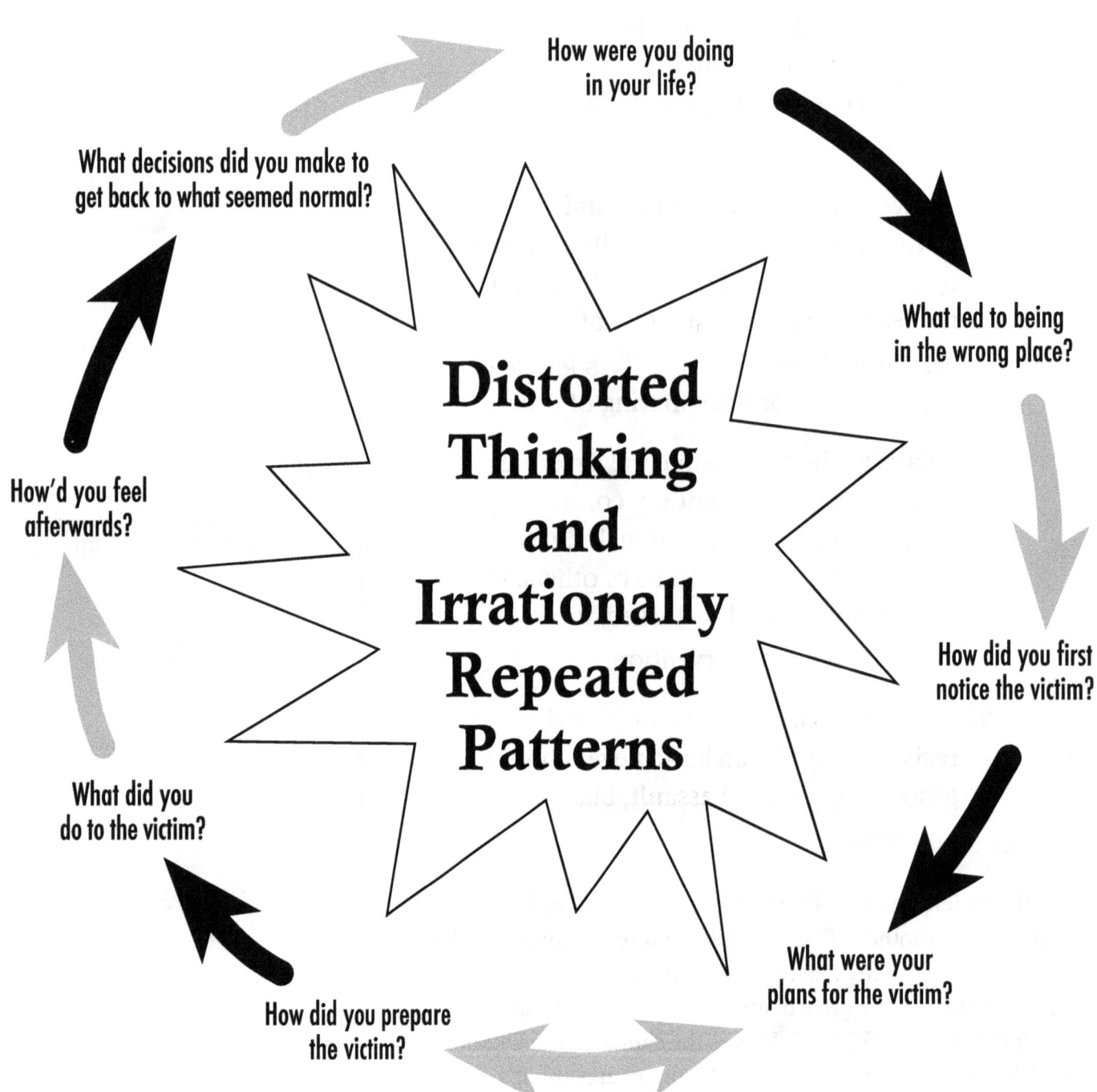

62

Lapse and Relapse

A relapse is "acting out" in the sense that I return to negative or problematic behaviors that do not fit into my life goals. These behaviors could be such as: lying, adultery, substance abuse, or smoking. In the case of sex offending, "relapse" means reenacting those behaviors which are sexual offenses.

Before any of us relapse (in any sense of the word) or reoffend in a sexual offense (in the legal sense) we experience a lapse. To best understand a lapse, we should closely examine its three part structure: motivation, permission giving, planning.

Lapse: Three-Part Structure

| **MOTIVATION:** sexually or socially deviant fantasy and arousal | **PERMISSION GIVING:** how we justify breaking our self-imposed rules | **PLANNING:** how, when, where; getting away with it, even fantasizing about how we might do it, etc |

Any one of the above is a lapse. Learning to distinguish lapses from normal sexuality is a great challenge for most offenders. For example, having a sexual thought is not, of itself, a lapse at all. Having a deviant thought is not a lapse. Only a deviant thought that puts you as an individual at risk is a lapse of the motivational kind.

Who has behavior that looks like lapses? Everyone. Children on a playground playing games like "Pirates," "Army," or "Cops and Robbers" are engaging in a play that toys with antisocial behaviors like pillaging, killing and robbing. Consider an adult nonsexual antisocial behavior like bank robbery. Upon seeing a cash drawer open up with rows of green bills, many have at some time fantasized about taking the money. For most of us this is a harmless fantasy. For people who rob banks a lot, it would be a lapse. When it comes to sexual behavior, who has not fantasized about inappropriate sexual behavior? Thus, we all need to increase our awareness of the MOTIVATION component of a lapse. This awareness is impossible without acceptance of both the normal fantasizing all humans engage in and the peculiar fantasizing that you may find attractive.

What has given me pleasure in the past will become a fantasy of the future. I may be out walking or watering the garden when I recollect some "golden oldie" of a sexual thought. To the degree that my fantasizing doesn't lead to antisocial or illegal behavior—no problem. But if it does…then, "Houston, we have a problem." Sexual thoughts and fantasies are normal—in the case of fantasies that take you to a dangerous place of increasing your likelihood of acting out, we recommend that you become so aware of your fantasies that you drop the dangerous ones within three seconds of their beginning and that you talk about them in group and with others in your support network.

What Feelings?

Why do counselors always ask you those inane questions about your feelings?

"How are you feeling today Mr. Jones?"

"What did that feel like for you Mr. Jones?"

"How do you feel about that feeling Mr. Jones?"

Counseling's dirty little secret is that we counselors really don't care about your feelings at all—at least no more than we do anyone else's. But there is a reason why we attempt to heighten your awareness of your feelings. Out of your awareness of your feelings comes an awareness of your needs. That awareness of your needs leads to an informed capacity to make decisions, as the following diagram illustrates.

So for the practicing alcoholic, he feels something (God knows what!), and he needs…a drink! So he makes a decision to amble down to the nearest watering hole. But imagine if you hadn't turned off your Personal Feeling Indicator after growing up in an alcoholic or similarly dysfunctional family or after your heart was broken by the fifteen failed relationships. Yes, you would feel pain, but you would also have access to vital information about yourself—your feelings. Then you could know what you needed and make better decisions as in: "I feel lonely, I need companionship, so I'll call a friend."

Feelings → Needs → Decisions

So how do we talk about these confusing feelings we've tried so hard to avoid? Won't we sound like wimps? In a strained relationship, wouldn't it be rude or abusive to share what I'm really feeling?

Well, it could be. Sometimes a little therapy can be a dangerous thing, as when I share, "I really feel that you're being an asshole." This is simply the abusive behavior known as name-calling with an "I feel" stuck on the front of it—a covert abusive statement, sometimes known as a "you" statement because even though it seems to be a vulnerable intimate statement about myself, it's not. It's a vicious judgment of the other person. Even counselors have been guilty of this in softly spoken sentences with a tone of concern like, "John, I feel that you're not really trying." Who are we to judge (in the sense of "condemn") another?

Instead, try a simple "I" statement.

"I feel angry when you treat me the way you're treating me."

"I feel unsure about whether or not you really love me."

"I feel nervous, uneasy and offended when you talk to me in that tone of voice."

All of us want to have emotionally intimate relationships that are safe and respectful. This emotional intimacy is similar to physical intimacy in that such intimacy contains within it the idea of "I'll show you mine if you show me yours." The "yours" and "mine" we're talking about in terms of emotional intimacy is our feelings. If you can't share your feelings when it's needed, then you don't get to ever have a satisfying level of emotional intimacy. This would make you far more at risk of acting out in an unacceptable way because you are repressing your normal human needs for love. In a similar way, your partner must also be capable of expressing his or her own feelings and listening to your feelings—otherwise, he or she will never be able to enjoy a loving, happy relationship.

> *"That which is **re**pressed will be **ex**pressed, inappropriately."*
> Author Unknown

Sexual Needs

What do humans need? Most people would give the simple answer of "food, water and shelter" without giving the matter much more thought; but perhaps more thought is necessary to understand humans, especially ourselves and why we do what we do. Alfred Adler came up with the idea that "All behavior is goal oriented." A boy who misbehaves in school may be acting out for a number of reasons such as trying to get his needs for attention met or trying to get a sense of power in his life (which might be otherwise full of feelings of powerlessness). In understanding sexual misbehavior we must consider the context of the acts and how else might the offender get his goals met legally and honorably. What was the goal of acting out sexually?

Perhaps the better question is not "what does the organism require in order to survive", but "what does the organism require in order to thrive." Clearly "food, water and shelter" is not enough of an answer. Everyone readily accepts that human beings are intellectual creatures with corresponding intellectual needs for education, mental stimulation, and a need for intellectual intimacy. In the same manner we find universal acceptance of the idea that humans have emotional needs, that children need love, affection, approval and so forth. Unless their needs are met, children and their normal development suffer. Human beings are physical beings with physical needs like food, water, sleep, light and exercise. But even lack of the later may not cause death; although it will certainly cause a failure to thrive in the sense that a lack of healthy exercise causes diminished strength and health.

In the same way humans are social beings with needs to associate and fellowship with others. They are spiritual beings with spiritual needs. In fact, the one and only dimension of the human experience where there is really any controversy at all about needs is in this area of human sexuality. Can't you just hear the objections, "Oh, c'mon, it's not like you're gonna die!" But we are talking about the failure to thrive, which could certainly lead to a diminished quality of life and perhaps even to premature death—at the very least causing profound unhappiness. You may in fact die emotionally.

This would be similar to our failure to get love. We may doubt our own need for love (or at least seriously minimize it), but none of us doubt a baby's need for love. By the time that baby has turned three, does he still need love? Of course. What about seven or ten years of age? Certainly he still needs love. Does he ever get to a point when he no longer needs love? If we were talking about your child, the answer would be very clear. Clearly, our children never outgrow their need for love. In the same way, neither do we. Our needs exist whether we are aware of them or not, whether we acknowledge them or not. They sometimes grow to a point where aware or not, we make terrible decisions out of sheer neediness that have equally terrible consequences.

So what are our sexual needs? You will hear much about this in the program, but certainly a partial list could include:

- Safety
- Respect for my gender, my body and my thoughts
- A need for physical release
- Age-appropriate sexual education
- Sexual intimacy and connectedness
- Sexual play
- A sense of acceptance for who I am sexually
- Sexual love
- A way of expressing my sexuality honorably

> "*That which is **re**pressed will be **ex**pressed, inappropriately.*"
> — Author Unknown

Any attempt to achieve recovery for offenders who have acted out sexually must include addressing these and other sexual needs—otherwise any plan of recovery is destined to fail miserably. You are a unique being. There is no one exactly like you in any of the ways that make you who you are—and that statement includes you as a sexual being. Failure to consider your personally unique sexual needs will ultimately lead to much unhappiness and additional acting out. Therefore our program will address this issue… repeatedly. Many of our clients find it helpful to remember:

"That which is **re**pressed will be **ex**pressed… inappropriately."
(Author Unknown)

Sexual Fantasies

Sexual fantasies are a normal part of everyone's sexuality. Many people are ignorant of this. They deny ever having sexual fantasies or include only those sexual thoughts which have not been consummated or lived out. This would be inaccurate. A fantasy (as opposed to a nightmare) is any sexual thought that gives pleasure. There are some rare moments when we have no sexual thoughts, such as when having the doctor perform some painful procedure. But just as humans are intellectual and emotional beings who have ideas and feelings most all the time, they are sexual beings with sexual feelings, urges, thoughts and fantasies almost all the time. We could imagine these sexual fantasies on a continuum starting with "0" indicating, for example, during one of those painful medical procedures that drive out all thoughts of any pleasure.

To the right of the illusory "0" we see "1," indicating **Spot Fantasies**, the lowest level of sexual fantasy. Spot fantasies are of the sort that occurs when one is driving down the street, sees an attractive person and feels a surge of longing to look again. This is expressive of sexual interest and a longing to connect with that person—at a fairly low level, but nevertheless it is expressive of sexual pleasure. This type of fantasy rarely lasts more than a few seconds and may occur multiple times in a day quite normally.

Next, at "2" we see **Fixed Image Fantasies**, which involve contemplation or looking for a longer period of time at a sexually gratifying image or sensation. Typical would be the male who is staring at a pornographic image in a magazine.

Next, at "3" is a **Sequence Fantasy**, which includes a series of fixed images (usually 3 to 5) repeated on an endless loop. An example would be remembering or imagining the arousing images or sensations associated with a sexually gratifying activity, such as the following: the first time I saw her that day, then seeing her take her clothes off, then touching her, then having intercourse, then ejaculating. This fantasy with its simple plot is a primitive precursor to the next type of fantasy which adds to the plot some dialogue or some reference to emotion.

At "4" is Narrative Fantasy. A narrative fantasy includes not only plot (what happened) but also dialogue, facial expressions and so forth that add depth to the fantasy, making it closer to what we might see in a pornographic film. A narrative fantasy tells a story that has a beginning, a middle and an end.

At "5" is a **Shared Narrative Fantasy**. It is the same as a narrative fantasy with the addition of actually sharing this with another though speech or in writing, in person or on the phone or the Internet.

At "6" is an **Acted-out Narrative Fantasy**, which would include those sexual experiences that some might refer to as "role-plays."

Why spend so much time and effort in identifying and cataloging sexual fantasies? This activity increases our awareness of fantasies as they occur and gives us language to discuss them—getting us to a point where we have our fantasies instead of our fantasies having us. This sense of perspective empowers us to guide our fantasies into healthy directions that give pleasure without putting us at risk of illegal and dishonorable sexual behaviors that violate law or individual conscience.

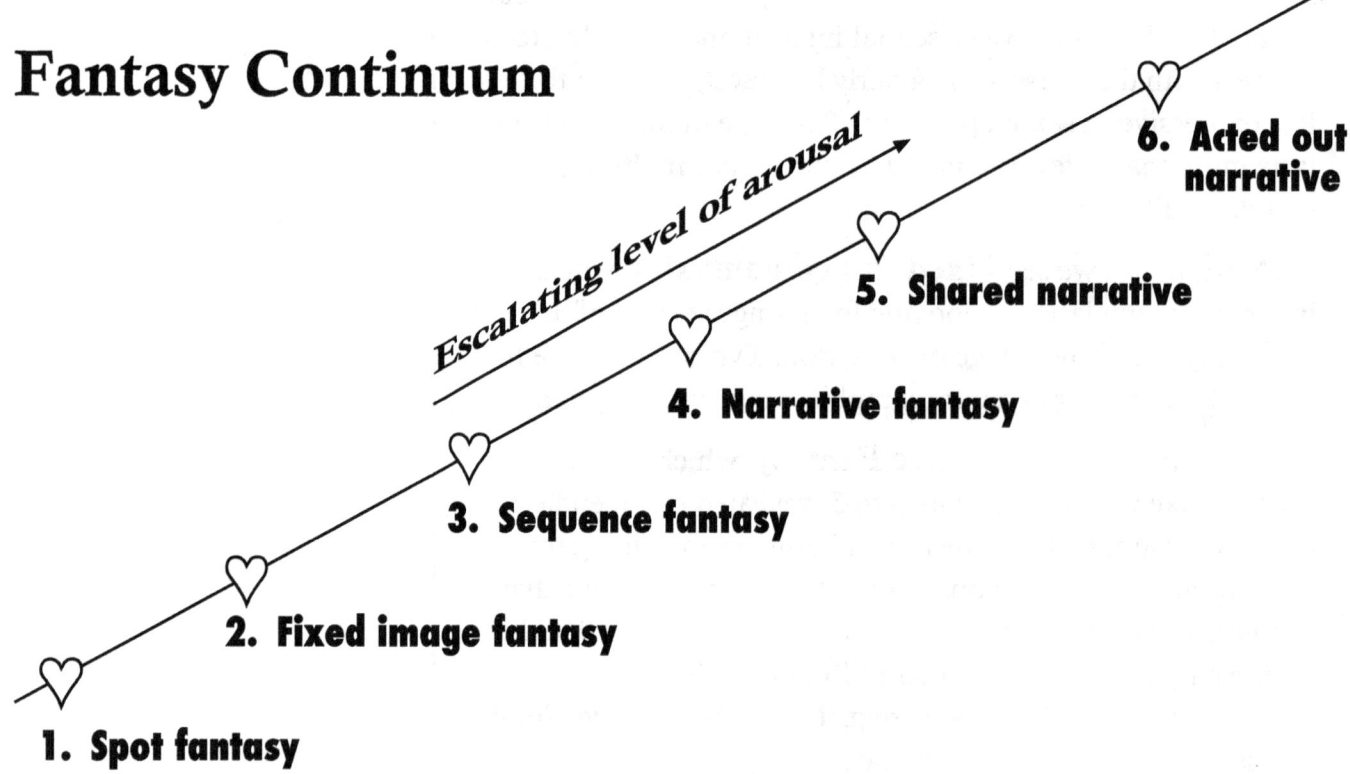

Fantasy Continuum

Escalating level of arousal

6. **Acted out narrative**
5. **Shared narrative**
4. **Narrative fantasy**
3. **Sequence fantasy**
2. **Fixed image fantasy**
1. **Spot fantasy**

Equality

Placement of this note was difficult because at first glance it seems that perhaps thoughts on equality should go into the "Changing My Thoughts" section—but most everyone knows that equality is politically correct and that one "should" believe in it. Perhaps the "Changing My Ways" section would be appropriate, but without changing one's heart about the idea of equality there is no possibility of actually having equality in a relationship.

A word here about what equality is not. Equality is not sameness. New research is constantly unearthing exciting and helpful information about the real and genuine differences between men and women. This research has improved and will continue to improve our appreciation for one another. This research has done much to mitigate the tremendous gender hostility and distrust that has been seen in 20th century American culture. Clearly equality in a relationship is not about working at the same job for the same pay as each other or even making the same financial contribution as one another to the family.

Equality in a relationship is fundamentally a question of respect. Equality in a relationship is an expression of the idea that we are both equally of value in this relationship. This results in the conviction that my masculine world view is valuable and contains the truth about the world—from a masculine viewpoint. In the same way, her feminine viewpoint is equally of value and shares truths that I in my masculine world cannot perceive. I alone see the world with a monocular vision—as does my mate when she is alone. Together we see the world binocularly and the depth and breadth of our vision is immeasurably increased.

Because of this fact of life, men and women need one another to be as successful as it is possible to imagine. Without my partner my view of the world from that other perspective, that unique perspective I will never have, is walled off from me. Couples have always had an advantage over individuals because they truly do have something that is more than the sum of their parts. His vision and her vision are only one and one. But together as a team they have a wholeness that is more than a list of the parts. She becomes my window on the world as women see it, I become her window as well and together, for the first time we see clearly the whole picture.

At least, we should. That we don't is far more common. Rather than sharing our views, rather than simply taking in the data from the other's unique perspective we argue about who's right. We compete and try to dominate the other. We each try to make the other in our own image.

"Why can't women see...?"

"Why do men have to be so....?"

The situation is a bit like the story of the blind men and the elephant, each arguing about who's right when in fact the blind man holding the elephant's tail ("It's like a rope.") is certainly just as right as the other blind man touching the elephant's leg ("It's like a column.").

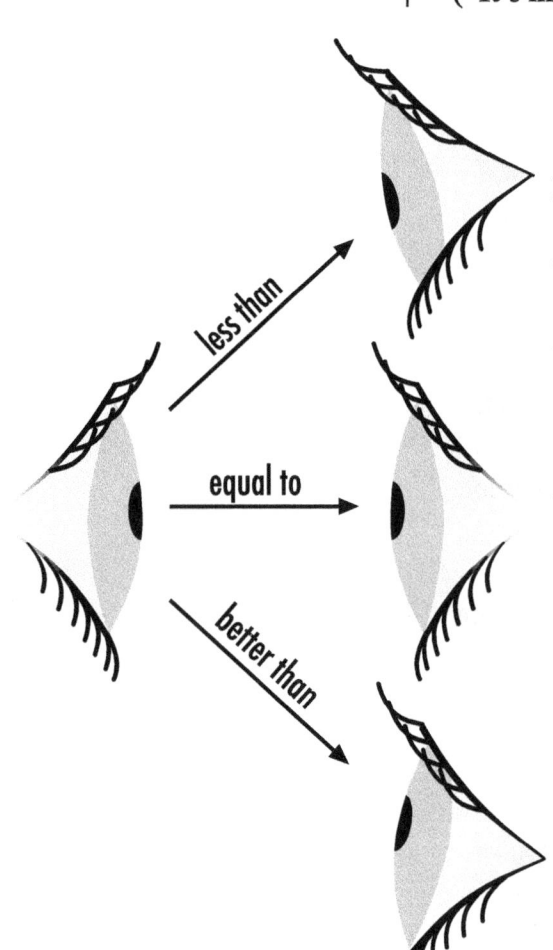

Getting to this place of respect is difficult. We must often overcome our irrational beliefs, childhood memories and romantic illusions. There are only three possible positions that I can have in relation to another. In the illustration, you (and your viewpoint) are represented by the solitary eyeball on the left. Others can either be your superior, looking down on you (however benignly) or they can be your inferior, looking up to you (resentfully or worshipfully) or they can be your equal.

The problem with having your partner function as your inferior is that she's not relating to you as a partner at all! You likely initiated the relationship with the Knight-In-Shining-Armor motif—therefore needing a damsel-in-distress. It seemed so wonderful at the beginning, didn't it? It seemed *so right*, being the big, strong confident one who was going to help her feel so safe and protected—what a sap! The female version of this is the woman who takes in stray dogs—the more needy and incompetent he is the more she finds him irresistible. The superior in this type of relationship functions as a parent—and it's lonely being a single parent.

The problem is simply reversed when your partner is actually your superior. It's hard for a grown man to be living with his mother again, isn't it? Talking down to you, correcting you like a small child, disrespecting you is bad enough—but did she have to do it in front of everyone else!

The only hope for any of us is equality. Only in a relationship based on equality can any two people hope to have a love that endures. Why? Because any adult functioning as a child in a relationship with their new adult parent is eventually going to resent the parent (as all teenagers eventually do), chafe under their control (no matter how well-intentioned) and then leave to find someone they can love as an equal (even if they only repeat the cycle). **Children don't like to have sex with their parents.** If your committed relationship is more like an adoption than a marriage, you will both end up frustrated with the situation and your sex life will reflect the relationship's distortion.

So there are three rules for starting out dating someone. We don't date people who are children running around in grown-up bodies. We only date people who have all of the following:

1. **A career**
   (not a MacJob, but a real plan for themselves)

2. **A residence**
   (no longer living with their parents)

3. **A car**
   (at least in those locales where most adults do have one)

Adherence to these rules will screen out a lot of the riff-raff. But it's only a start. You are still responsible for doing the sophisticated follow-up interviews of future applicants seeking a leading role in your life.

Compatibility

If you buy the idea about equality and you've gone to all the trouble to date only grown-ups, sooner or later you're going to fall in love. You're in for some grand feelings; this is a great time—go ahead and enjoy the rush. BUT don't for one minute buy into the irrational thought that because you love one another that therefore you're meant to be together. There are other considerations (see Narcissistic Love which follows this section). Being in love with someone is only one of several necessary but insufficient conditions for having a great relationship. A commitment to an abuse-free lifestyle would be another. But there are other issues, some of which could be termed "deal breakers." If you're a nonsmoker, another person's smoking habit might be a deal breaker. Drug abuse, destructive alcohol habits, irresponsible financial management, and other issues seem pretty obvious deal breakers—but millions have had to learn this the hard way.

Please consider the notion of compatibility. Other people may be absolutely fabulous—but not for you. For example, if you're a morning person and the other person just isn't, you may find yourself having breakfast alone the rest of your life. Not a big deal, you say. Well, ask anyone who's been married a while and you'll find that sometimes the smallest things become very big (and tiresome) after ten or twenty years.

Another issue would be whether or not you're an introvert or an extrovert. This issue has nothing to do with shyness. There are shy extroverts and very outgoing introverts. This issue has nothing to do with friendliness or liking people. Some of the most misanthropic people in the world are extroverts...or introverts. The question is: are you the kind of person who recharges your batteries when you're in a crowd or when you're alone? If your mate is the opposite of you, you may find yourself pressured to go out on the town just when you were looking forward to a little down time. How many marriages does that sound like?

When it comes to affection—on a scale of one to ten, if ten is the most affectionate person you've ever observed—what are you? Go ahead and pick your number. This number is unlikely to ever change in a person's lifetime. Then pose this question to the one you're in love with. If your two answers are very different from one another you two may find one of you is always feeling needy while the other is always feeling smothered. Threes (on a scale of ten) are not inferior to eights, this is not a moral issue. It's a compatibility issue. You may still be in love with the other person, but consider loving them from across town. You might both be in love—but happier with someone else.

There are lots of issues relating to compatibility: your vision of your future lifestyle and your desired future sex life (funny how so many people considering a sexually committed relationship never actually break down and talk about sex). If your partner wants a simple little life and you're dreaming of striking it rich and traveling the world—your visions are incompatible. If your partner loves, loves, loves sex and just has to have it— once a year—you may have an incompatibility problem.

These are not love problems—you may already love one another. But you can love people who are really not good for you, can't you? Most of us have already found that out.

Letting go of a wonderful person—who's just not right for you—takes a lot of maturity. Letting go of a person who's wonderful (for someone else) is a strategic decision one makes to have a good life, as opposed to the immediate gratification of "just having someone." These kinds of mature decisions hurt at first, but not over time, and they get easier to make the more mature we become.

Intimacy Skills— A Technical Approach to Getting My Needs for Love Met

It would come as a surprise to many, but sexual deviancy is not the most common characteristic of sex offenders. The far more common trait is an extreme inability to get the individual's needs for love and connectedness met in an honorable and legal manner. Nearly all sex offenders have these intimacy skill deficits. There should be little surprise in this in that people who commit sexual offenses have usually been reared by parents who have difficulty in getting their own needs met—so how could they have passed on information they themselves never had.

There are many skills but the basics every individual should have are (in order of increasing difficulty): 1) the basic knowledge of social norms and courtesy; 2) is able to identify feelings; 3) can make normal eye contact and introduce self and acknowledge others; 4) is honoring of others and respectful, non-abusive; 5) can make small talk; 6) can set boundaries; 7) generates and maintains social network; 8) becomes willing to risk relationships in order to possibly save relationships; 9) defends boundaries effectively; 10) terminates unhelpful relationships; 11) enjoys intimacy without drama and willingly makes intimate disclosures.

Using an erasable pencil, chart your own perception of your skills on the chart on the next page, using "10" to indicate a very high level of skill and "1" to indicate a very low level. Share this with your treatment provider and others you wish to understand you. This exercise will help you narrow your scope of confusion and focus your efforts to grow in an extremely effective manner. The chart will also help you identify the strengths and weaknesses of others with whom you are trying to have a relationship.

Intimacy Skill Set
(Technical approach to getting my needs for love met.)

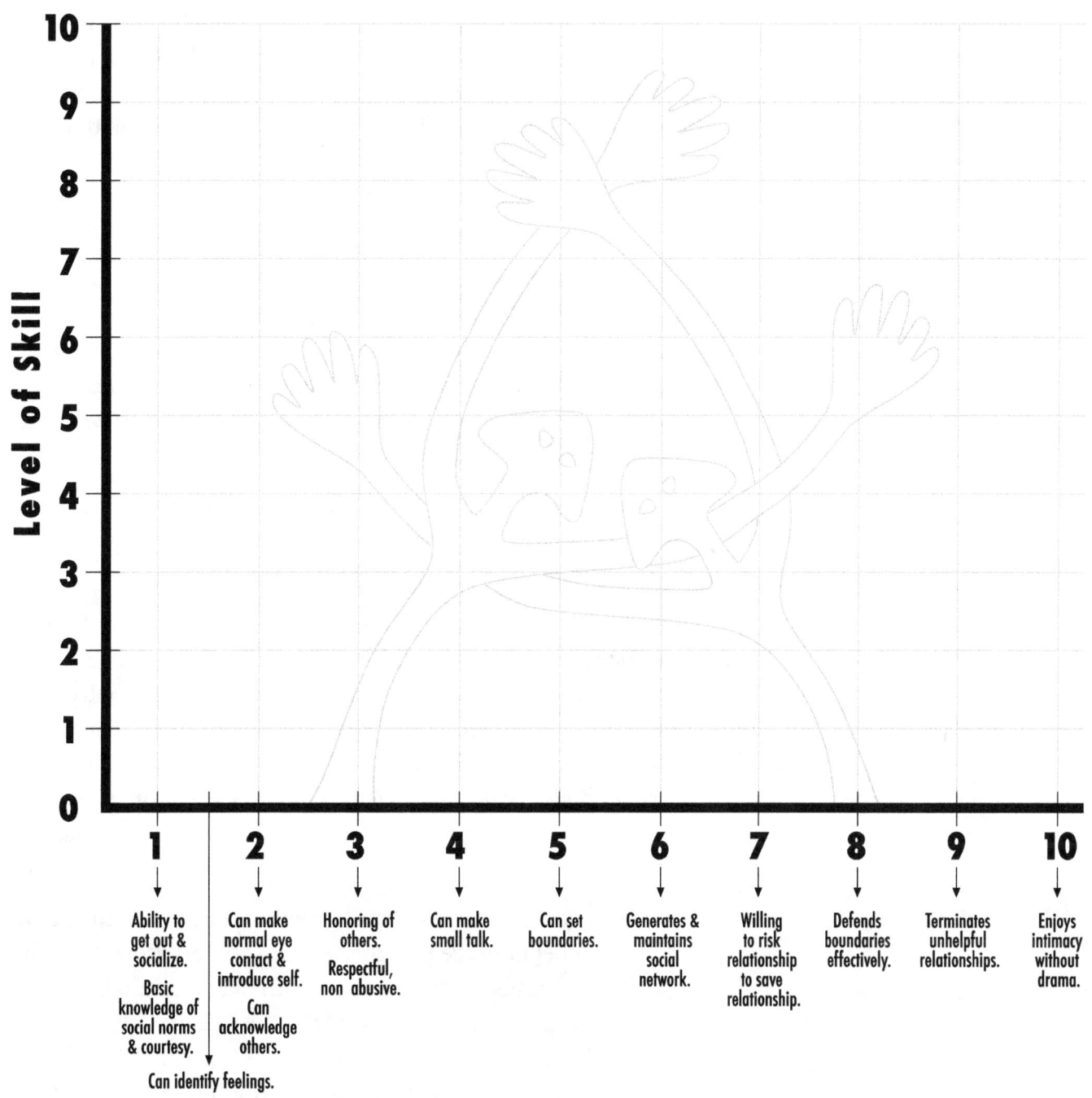

Level of skill (y-axis: 0–10)

1. Ability to get out & socialize. Basic knowledge of social norms & courtesy.
2. Can make normal eye contact & introduce self. Can acknowledge others. Can identify feelings.
3. Honoring of others. Respectful, non abusive.
4. Can make small talk.
5. Can set boundaries.
6. Generates & maintains social network.
7. Willing to risk relationship to save relationship.
8. Defends boundaries effectively.
9. Terminates unhelpful relationships.
10. Enjoys intimacy without drama.

Narcissistic Love Timeline

"Love at first sight" is not lust, at least not entirely. This love is that first intoxicating rush of genuine feeling for another that typically precedes all successful relationships. Unfortunately it precedes all the unsuccessful ones as well. It would be disastrous to conclude that because I am "in love" with someone that I really love them at all. And how could I love them anyway—in the first days of a relationship I don't even know them, much less love them. I can never love someone until I know them.

How does this work? When I initially fall in love what I am most aware of is how much the other person and I have in common. She embodies my values, shares my interests and even, oh my God, even has the looks that target my brain's pleasure centers in a way that resonates as "true." You can hear this when she talks to her friends:

"I just met the greatest guy. He is so (fill in this blank with something she finds priceless as a man) and he actually likes to (do what I like or find priceless in a man).

The guy says or thinks similar thoughts about her looks, her ways, her interests, her morals and so forth. Once I've fallen in love I find the other person pretty much perfect. And why shouldn't I—the other person is a reflection of myself and their similarity to me, no—her identical reflection of me is very easy to love and accept because, well, she is...a refection of me. What I love about her is what I love about me. That's what we mean by narcissism.

This pink cloud of endless bliss begins to fray over time and eventually I begin to see that this person—otherwise absolutely perfectly me—is also a, sniff, person with her own mind. Where I like this (as all right thinking people do), she likes that. I am pro something-or-other and she, against all reasonable expectation, is con. We begin to argue, not too much at first, but with increasing dismay (either expressed aloud or passively contained within) I find we seem to be drifting apart. Well, the simple truth is we are not drifting apart, we were never together in the first place.

It is at precisely this point in the relationship that I begin to see that she is so much more than my mere reflection, she is her own person. From that moment on what we have is the opportunity to learn to actually love one another for who we are, just as we really are. We usually fail at this because it's hard to love people, they are so...different. Different from me, different from the way I think people should live and do things. Sigh. Most of us never mature enough that we can really love someone enough to live with them as they are. We usually end up loving the person they could potentially be,

"It would be so great if he [or she] could just...[be and do as I want]."

The timeline below tells you precisely when narcissistic love begins to end and its pink cloud begins to darken. This darkening could be the beginning of true love—or not. True love is that kind of mature love where we truly love the person for who they are—whether we live with them or not. It's hard to be this mature. The odds are heavily against you ever making it, sigh, but you have to try.

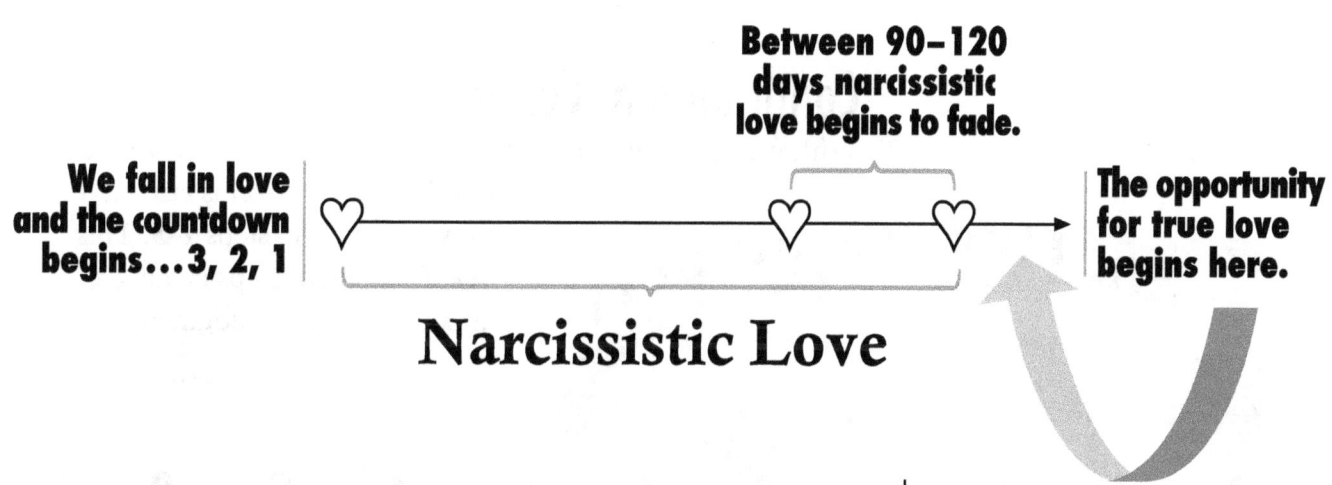

Commitment

Often one hears something like, "He's a nice guy, but he just can't commit." The remark is meant as a criticism when said by either gender. The criticism is based on an irrational idea: that commitment in relationships is a matter of all or nothing, that commitment is a black or white issue. This use of the word "commitment" in relationships is similar to the use of the word "trust" with a used car salesman in a pressured sale. "What, don't you trust me?" The implication is that one is "bad" for not trusting. In a similar manner a would-be mate can paint me as "bad" for not giving her the particular commitment she's looking for. Men do the same thing.

This way of looking at commitment makes it easy to manipulate and to be manipulated and it makes life extremely uncomfortable and nonsensical. We look at acquaintances and friends differently and feel as though we have greater commitments to some than to others—and rightfully so. Rather than looking at commitment as an "all or nothing" proposition we should consider how it would look on a continuum like the one here.

Continuum of Commitment

With friends we go through steps sequentially; but if we are lonely enough or the other person is attractive enough—we often skip steps 1–5. This leapfrogging of steps creates anxiety and poor judgment.

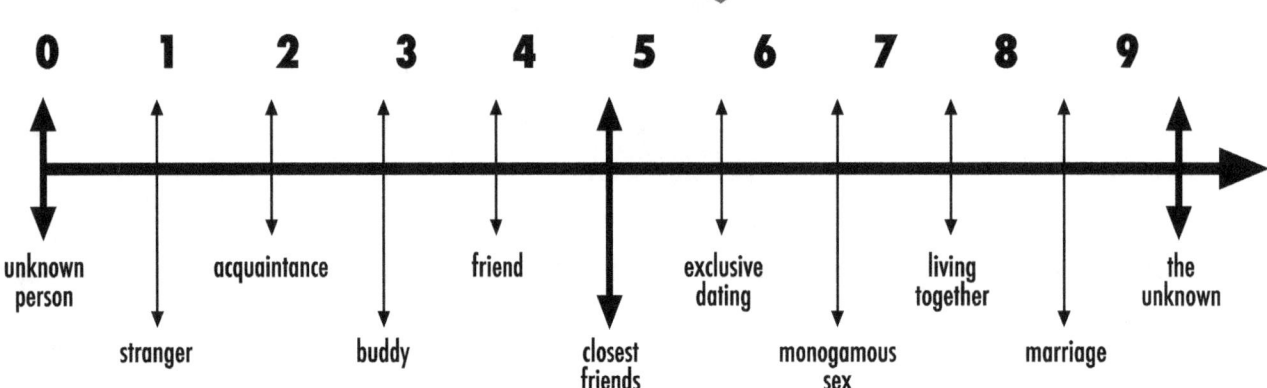

(While looking at the chart, consider the depth of your commitments in the following scenarios. Remember, sex can occur at virtually any level of commitment—the choice is yours.)

Continuum of Commitment

0—When one considers the "unknown people" of the world, the commitment to them is as close to "0" as can be imagined.

1—Even with strangers most civilized people feel as though these are owed "common decency" and "common courtesy." For examples: aid to the fallen, public courtesies and so forth.

2—Our acquaintances get all of the above, plus those commitments which total strangers do not get—small amounts of information about our lives, small amounts of money, time or other resources as needed.

3—Buddies (like those at work) are those who have gone beyond mere acquaintance; they get all of the above plus a commitment for more money, time and other resources like emotional investments such as the time and trouble to confront.

4—Friends, yes, get all of the above plus even more money, time and resources. Friends get genuine, sincere and nearly complete emotional access to our real opinions and real confrontations—even when we risk losing the relationship. Friends get higher levels of confidentiality with us. Friends get an honest answer to "How ya doin'?"

5—Closest friends get all the money, time and resources available. They get maximum emotional investment. Maximum confrontation and confidentiality. My close inner circle of friends deserve the truth and nothing but.

6—Exclusive dating, it could be argued, would only be made after all the other stages have been passed and includes all the other levels of commitment. The commitment is that his person is not merely a recreational interest; this is someone we're considering as a life partner. The commitment includes a commitment to "break up" honorably.

7—Monogamous sex could be at this stage or later, depending on your beliefs. The commitment includes a mutual commitment to get all of my sexual needs met through the other and a commitment to meet the other's needs. Obviously a deeper commitment than what we have with our closest friends.

8—Living together implies a much deeper level of commitment in terms of finances and respecting one another along with all of the other commitments mentioned above.

9—Marriage. All of the above. Plus the vows(!)—for life! No wonder some people turn to drink!

10—The unknown. Here do dragons dwell.

The Abuse-free Lifestyle

In our culture, behaviors like yelling, name-calling and using an intimidating tone are normalized and considered "just the way it is" or an acceptable consequence for bad behavior. But is such behavior really normal? Do you really want to have it in your relationships, especially your intimate ones? Do you want this behavior in your home? When considered as a choice, rather than a normal inevitability like death and taxes, abusive behavior becomes an option in life that most of us could do without.

But is it possible to have an abuse-free lifestyle? When we consider abusive behavior as an outcome "caused" by past experiences ("He grew up in an abusive home and that's why he does that."), poverty, ignorance, the abuse of others, alcoholism and substance abuse and so forth, then we miss the HUGE reality that abuse is not caused by anything, it is a choice. I choose to call someone a name. Statements like "She made me, she drove me to it." Or "She knows how to push my buttons." only rob me of responsibility for my own behavior, putting the other person in the driver's seat of my life. This way of thinking robs me of my power to have the kind of relationships I want, to lead the kind of life I want. This is unacceptable.

Success in your program with us will be impossible if you are unable to achieve an abuse-free lifestyle. Good relationships are an essential part of your future success. You will never have satisfying, loving relationships if you allow for the presence of abuse. Even if the abuse is only intermittent or relatively low level. How good can your relationship or your home life be if you are getting disrespected even intermittently?

What are the steps to achieving an abuse-free lifestyle?

1. Make a personal commitment to attaining and living an abuse-free life. No one can do this for you and it is an achievable goal for everyone.
2. Talk about my goal to the important people in my personal life.
3. Learn what is abusive behavior so that I can identify it as soon as possible after it occurs.

4. Grow more sensitive to abuse so that I can identify it when it occurs.

5. Apologize to the victim for my every instance of abusive behavior.

6. Require apologies from those who treat me abusively.

7. Terminate relationships with those who cannot or will not learn to treat me respectfully and surround myself with those who can.

Your group will help you achieve each stage of this process and coach you as needed.

Fair Fighting

Most sex crimes grow out of a basic inability to have normal human needs for love, intimacy and sexual gratification met in ways that are both legal and honorable. That reality leaves us to look for getting our needs met dishonorably and illegally.

One of the most common failings in our search for satisfying relationships is our attempt to keep whatever beginnings of a relationship we might have by doing as much as we can to please the other person. This overreaching attempt to please the other is a pathological attempt at people-pleasing that leaves no room for me to make room in the relationship for myself.

Ultimately the other person comes to see that I am engaging in some serious ass-kissing and, as a consequence of that awareness, loses respect for me. This makes my attempts at doing whatever it takes to save the relationship into the very behavior that causes me to lose the relationship.

Paradoxically, in order to save the relationship, I must first become willing to lose the relationship. The first concept you'll be asked to learn in this regard is that: *"Conflict is an essential and inevitable part of every intimate relationship."*

> *"Conflict is an essential and inevitable part of every intimate relationship."*

Conflict (or fighting, or arguing, or disagreeing—whatever we call it) is the way we resolve the problems that keep us from feeling safe and relaxed with one another. What's so scary about conflict is that most of us have seen conflicts go nowhere and believe that conflict itself is the problem. This is an irrational belief; conflict is not the problem. It is the way you've been conflicting that is the problem. You will be taught in your groups how to fight or argue according to rules that ensure success.

The Rules for Fair Fighting

1. **No abuse**
2. **By mutual consent**
3. **Any one subject**

These rules will be reviewed at length in your program, but essentially: the first rule pertains to always maintaining respectful behavior and language; the second states that we never just start fighting—all fights are planned and scheduled (just like any important activity involving others' time); the third rule asserts that we can fight about anything, let's just address issues one at a time, solving one before we proceed to another.

Of course, both parties must agree to these rules. Single people are at an advantage here because they can dump anyone who can't get with the program. Singles don't have the investment of time, money and sometimes children that those already in committed relationships have.

For those in committed relationships, they must realize that no relationship can be good unless it is first safe. Again, unless we "pass" safe, we cannot get to good. If you are in a relationship that is ever disrespectful of you, then your home is not a safe place. In fact, for home to be home it must first be a safe place. That is what we mean by the word "home."

Is This Relationship Working?

Evaluating a relationship's value to you is essential to knowing whether or not you'd best stay or leave. Most people seem to use the following criteria for staying:

"But I still love her."

This statement is based on the irrational belief that love and love alone is what is required for success in a relationship. In dysfunctional relationships this nonsense usually results in people staying until all the love is stomped into the ground and is dead forever. Yikes.

A more rational view would be that love is a necessary but insufficient part of a successful adult relationship. Other parts of the relationships are also essential—like respect, compatibility and attraction, to name just some of the essentials.

Cultivating the ability to evaluate a relationship in a detached, adult manner greatly increases your chances of success. The confusing global nature of words like "love" doesn't help in cultivating this detached evaluation of a relationship. Thankfully, there are tools for promoting this sort of thinking. Rather than thinking about love in the global sense, let's consider successful intimacy as a function of success along a small list of continuums—specifically, let us consider a successful relationship as a function of feeling safe. Everyone knows what the feeling of "safe" feels like.

- Running for home plate in an elementary school game of kickball and getting there before being tagged with the ball "you're safe."
- Fleeing a bully only to run into a favorite teacher, parent or BIG best friend feels safe.
- After being with someone who didn't accept you at all, to meet (finally) someone who does.

Dennis Bagarozzi has written a book called *Enhancing Intimacy In Marriage (2001)* that offers some idea about looking at relationships in a helpful way. Mr. Bagarozzi has developed a list of dimensions that make up a significant part of any relationship and the following work uses his list. We have modified his ideas a bit in order to create a tool for you to use in evaluating your past (and present!) relationships. First, here are the dimensions of intimacy we will examine—with the definitions we shall use.

1. Financial Intimacy—the ability to safely discuss money issues with my partner.

2. Emotional Intimacy—the ability to safely share my feelings with my partner.

3. Intellectual Intimacy—the ability to safely share my ideas with my partner.

4. Physical (nonsexual) Intimacy—the ability to safely share space or proximity with my partner.

5. Aesthetic Intimacy—the ability to safely share beauty with my partner.

6. Social Intimacy—the ability to safely share socializing with my partner.

7. Recreational Intimacy—the ability to safely have fun with my partner.

8. Historical Intimacy—the ability to safely share my past with my partner.

9. Sexual Intimacy—the ability to safely share my sexuality (not necessarily sex and certainly not exclusively intercourse) with my partner. Rape, for example, is sexual—but never intimate because it is not safe.

10. Spiritual Intimacy—the ability to safely share my spirituality with my partner. This is not the same as being identical in spirituality—such as two fundamentalists might conclude. Intimacy is about feeling safe with the differences too.

Of course, the partner must also be able to safely share with me for there to be intimacy. Also, sharing my feelings or emotional intimacy, is not about merely sharing my pleasant feelings like "I love you." Emotional intimacy includes sharing (and feeling safe sharing) my feelings like,

- "Sometimes I feel unsure about our relationship."
- "Today I don't feel loved or valued."
- "Right now I'm just really mad at you."

These expressions, along with the ones we love to hear, are equally important in forming a truly intimate relationship with another—to feeling safe being myself with my mate.

Use the following chart to evaluate your past (and then later, your current) relationship in order to more fully understand just what went wrong. How much intimacy you need in order to feel content with a relationship is up to you—some people report they don't need to hit on all nine cylinders of the intimacy engine, others report they are unwilling to give up on any of the nine—they want them all. Some people rank the relationship alone and later ask their current partner to do the same. They then compare their perceptions of the relationship. To their lasting joy of course.

Circle the number that best describes your situation: "0" indicates "no intimacy" and "10" indicates "as much as you could ever imagine or have ever observed."

1. Financial intimacy   0   1   2   3   4   5   6   7   8   9   10

2. Emotional Intimacy   0   1   2   3   4   5   6   7   8   9   10

3. Intellectual Intimacy   0   1   2   3   4   5   6   7   8   9   10

4. Physical Intimacy   0   1   2   3   4   5   6   7   8   9   10

5. Aesthetic Intimacy   0   1   2   3   4   5   6   7   8   9   10

6. Social Intimacy   0   1   2   3   4   5   6   7   8   9   10

7. Recreational Intimacy   0   1   2   3   4   5   6   7   8   9   10

8. Historical Intimacy   0   1   2   3   4   5   6   7   8   9   10

9. Sexual Intimacy   0   1   2   3   4   5   6   7   8   9   10

10. Spiritual Intimacy   0   1   2   3   4   5   6   7   8   9   10

Recommended Films

If one is easily offended, the following list will give plenty of opportunities for distress. The list is offered not to sensationalize or disturb, but rather the opposite. Our desire in providing these suggestions is to promote thoughtful conversation between adults about sex. The commentary available on the DVD's is often very helpful. For those offended by any sexual content, there are no materials that will not offend.

Films:

- *Kinsey*, starring Liam Neeson. A film that documents the revolutionary work of Alfred Kinsey and the difficulties of our society's discussing any sexual topics.
- *Secretary*, starring James Spader. This film, without any sex or violence, describes kinky sexual behaviors as possible adaptations to more conventional but also more dysfunctional alternatives.
- *Happiness*. An intelligent and fairly graphic depiction of multiple offenders and their cycles of abuse.
- *The Woodsman*, starring Kevin Bacon. The story of a convicted child molester upon his release from prison.
- *LIE or long Island Express*. A homosexually oriented story of exploitation of young teens.
- *Mystic River*. Starring Sean Penn and Tim Robbins. Portrays life-long aftereffects of severe abuse.
- *Sleepers*. Starring Brad Pitt and Kevin Bacon. The trauma of abuse as played out in adult lives.
- *Marnie*. A classic Hitchcock film with Tippi Hedren in a serious exploration of sexual abuse.
- *Mysterious Skin*. A look at the long-term effects of childhood sexual abuse.
- *Don Jon*. Starring Joseph Gordon-Levitt. More than any other film depicts the vast gulf between a life based on intimacy and titillation compared to those having titillation alone.

Contact Information

We welcome your contacting us as we are always looking to improve this manual. If you have ideas that you think could help or want to provide your feedback, please do so.

Our email address is:
    support@stevening.com

Our mailing address is:
    ICI
    3500 Lakeside Court, Suite 130
    Reno, Nevada 89509

Steven Ing uses his almost three decades of experience as a therapist to create a safe space for people to talk about sexuality. He does this by proactively communicating with different groups — regional church groups about integrating sexuality and spirituality, journalists about asking the right questions when investigating stories about sexuality, HR representatives about creating a healthy workplace culture, parents about talking to kids about sex, military members about domestic violence — and he has worked alongside police and government to recommend rational, effective policies about sex offenders and human trafficking. All with the goal of helping people manage their sexuality intelligently.

        For more information visit

        StevenIng.com

 Steven Ing is a Marriage and Family Therapist whose clinical work with sex offenders has resulted in an extremely low recidivism rate. Clinician and author, he presents regularly as an expert on the treatment of sex offenders. As a consultant, he has developed community-wide action plans that address sex offending as a public health problem. He is the author of the book *We're All Like This: Learning to Talk about Our Human Sexual Needs*.

ING Intellectual, Inc.
3500 Lakeside Court, Suite 130 • Reno, Nevada 89509
support@stevening.com

www.ingramcontent.com/pod-product-compliance
Lightning Source LLC
Chambersburg PA
CBHW080348170426
43194CB00014B/2719